SEE NO
EVIL

L. Sydney Fisher

The Write Publishing Group, Inc.

Other Books by L. Sydney Fisher

STANDALONES
See No Evil

The Phoenix Series
The Phoenix Mission, Part I
The Phoenix Codes, Part II

The Bradford Series
The Haunting of Natalie Bradford, Part I
The Haunting of Natalie Bradford, Part II:
Waking the Dead
The Haunted Prophecy of Natalie
Bradford:
The Complete Bradford Series

The Haunted
The Haunted: A Haunted History Series,
Volume I

Join Sydney's Newsletter
@http://www.LSydneyFisher.com

And remember,

Sleep With The Lights ON!

Author's Note

See No Evil is a story inspired by TRUE EVENTS. While the settings in the story are real life locations that have been recreated to match the time of the event, some of the characters are the author's creation. When appropriate, the author has dramatized some scenes in this book for the sake of storytelling.

Copyright, 2016 by L. Sydney Fisher

All rights reserved. No part of this book may be reproduced or transmitted in any form or by any means, electronic or mechanical, including photocopying, recording, or by any information storage and retrieval system, without permission in writing from the copyright owner.

Editing provided by: The Write Publishing Group, Inc.

Book Cover Design: The Write Publishing Group, Inc.

*With a special thanks to Debra Barton for Cover Images

ISBN-13: 978-1537099620
ISBN-10: 1537099620

Trademark Copyright, 2016

Dedicated to...

Hannah & Bryce

My True Love

With Special Thanks to...

Amanda H. Viator

Introduction

This story has been percolating in the recesses of my mind since 2013. After my debut novel *The Haunting of Natalie Bradford* was released, I had the honor of speaking to a crowd of enthusiastic readers and paranormal fans at the Dixie Regional Library located in Pontotoc, Mississippi. Unbeknown to me was the town's very own psychic celebrity of the 20th century known as Seymour Prater, a man often referred to as The Mississippi Mystic.

The Library Director, Regina Graham approached me with the Prater story as I was preparing to leave that day. She told me about a man from Pontotoc who was known to have a unique gift that enabled him to find lost objects. She also advised me that his fame spread far and wide across the southeast earning him notoriety as a "fortune teller", a label that his wife highly detested.

Stories of Seymour Prater covered the inside pages of newspapers and magazines from time to time. Fortunately, some of these articles had been saved and collected by the library. Mrs. Graham invited me to explore the supernatural wonder and offered to help any way that she could.

Fast forward almost two years later to January, 2016. I had just released my supernatural bestseller, *The Phoenix Mission* a month earlier. That book was inspired by the U.S. Army's psychic spy program, Stargate. And while my creative tone was fixed on that material, the Prater story easily came to mind as a project that I needed to explore.

After meeting with Mrs. Graham who provided me with the Seymour Prater file of newspaper clippings and family journals, I began my research into the man who often called himself "the man with the radio mind". I sat at a long, conference table inside a room designated for Genealogy research and slowly flipped through the newspapers one page at a time, taking it all in. I was mesmerized. Seymour Prater and his story was more than I had anticipated, and I knew that most people in the area probably didn't realize how profound his ability was and what it all meant. He was destined to be a legend.

As someone who has studied the paranormal and unexplained most of my life, I realized the magnitude of his gift within seconds of picking up that first newspaper article. My mind raced with thoughts of past explorations. There was another man who I studied over the years, and he possessed the same abilities as Prater, but this man became known worldwide. His name was Edgar Cayce, The Sleeping Prophet, and I knew that in order to study Seymour Prater, I needed to study Edgar Cayce one more time. Don't miss my addition of *The Divinely Gifted* at the end of this book.

See No Evil is a project that included detailed research. This research even included studying the flow of the Tombigbee River and the riverboats that traveled to Aberdeen during the time of Seymour Prater's boyhood. It was on that fateful day in Aberdeen, Mississippi when Prater met the man who would deliver a message that shaped the course of his life. The entire Prater story is laced with providence and even what some may define as predestination. Pay attention to the opening scenes that have been created most likely as they happened. Unknown until now, Lewis Prater became Seymour Prater's father *only* because Thomas Jefferson Brown was captured and taken prisoner at the Battle of Missionary Ridge in November, 1863. Fate?

While parts of this story have been dramatized for the sake of storytelling, let it be known that this really happened. On January 3, 1931, Arthur Floyd was murdered at his store in Carrollton, Mississippi. And as the town lived in terror from the haunting at the Floyd place, Seymour Prater became the victim's only hope for solving a murder and putting the angry spirit to rest. While the town's folk frantically searched for answers, it was *murder at first sight* for The Mississippi Mystic.

The Praetor's Eyes

He sees; you don't.
He knows; you won't.
The future and past before us lay,
What you don't know is why.
Tangible and intangible, whisper and weave,
Thoughts dance around and then they too leave.
The Captain, he charts a course, Oh so true!
Unfortunately, it's not clear to me or to you.
Praetor states, I'll guide, suggest, and inform, but
it's your choice to accept or remain forlorn.
Only some can see earth's nonlinear thoughts,
And fewer still what under heaven is wrought.
Praetor knows, and he will share, but it's your
choice... The truth awaits only if you dare.

Written by: Amanda H. Viator

Chapter 1

Missionary Ridge. Chattanooga, Tennessee
November 25, 1863
3:00 p.m.

The sound of footsteps sliding across the grassy slope alerted the Rebel forces of an impending attack as the Federals charged up the side of the mountain, their boots heavy and marred with mud formulated from the recent rain. As they pushed forward into Confederate territory, they began to shout, their roars echoing across the side of the ridge.

"Chickamauga! Chickamauga!" The Federals chanted in unison.

Confederate General Braxton Bragg stared into the face of certain victory, his deep brown eyes moistened by the chilling blast that swept over his face and caused him to step backwards. It was a warning; a cold harbinger alerting him of the end as he quickly began to order his men's retreat. But the order came too late as the federal troops advanced. The Yankees had begun to charge the ridge without the order from Union General Thomas George. They had taken the advance under their own promissory and burst forth with a force so powerful that thousands of men fell to their deaths. Haunting screams could be heard as bodies tumbled hundreds of feet down the hillside while others found their graves where they fell.

Blood splattered in every direction as bullets split skulls and severed carotid arteries. The bloody death found its mark upon the hands of some of the men still standing who, in a desperate attempt to save their best friend's life, dragged the lifeless body until their own need to survive forced them into abandonment.

Thomas Jefferson Brown, 34th Alabama Infantry Regiment, Company B, fell to his knees. He grimaced in pain as his kneecaps hit the rocky slag surface. His feet cramped inside his boots and his arms trembled from fatigue. He held his musket tight, his head lowered and his eyes closed as he felt the enemy's encirclement.

Just as the enemy's shouts rang loud, he felt a quick, hard thrust from the bottom of a boot. The Yankee kicked him breathless and sent his body forward as he slammed face first into the rock. The tender skin of his left brow split open and began to bleed, the blood trickling into his eye socket.

"Get up, Soldier. Get up and fight." The Yankee mocked him and attempted to roll his body over with his foot.

Thomas Jefferson Brown was not near death, but he might as well been. He was now a captured Confederate soldier and a prisoner of war to the Federals. Seconds seemed like hours as his mind played back the conversation that he had with his best friend, Lewis Meadow Prater who was serving with him. Both men had enlisted in Coosa County, Alabama. The regiment was organized April 15, 1862 and then moved to Tupelo, Mississippi and placed under General Arthur M. Manigault's Brigade.

Prater and Brown had it made in Tupelo. The camp was well-guarded and food was plentiful. They were positioned on the east side in a Confederate camp that housed several hundred men overlooking the city. It was on this hillside where Prater and Brown ate their evening supper of corn, salt pork, and bread while sitting around the glowing campfires that could be seen almost a mile away near General Bragg's headquarters. The Tupelo camps were a part of what became known as the "Black Prairie" because of its fertile land. Crops were easily grown in abundance and livestock was plentiful. Thus, Tupelo and its region were capable of feeding the entire Confederate Army of the West.

On the evening before Prater and Brown were set to depart for Chattanooga, Brown unknowingly revealed a man's destiny. During the evening meal, he nudged his friend, Lewis

Prater while both men finished the last of their bread rations.

"Lewis, my good friend, I have an urgent request of you and beg for your consent." Thomas Jefferson Brown locked eyes with his closest friend as he thought of his wife back in Coosa County, Alabama. What would happen to Martha if she became a widow? How would she raise their two sons alone? Prater was his first consideration. Although Prater was nineteen years old, he had never married and had no children.

Prater looked intently at Brown as he broke a piece of bread. "Yes, of course. What is it?"

Brown looked away and hesitated for a brief moment as he collected his thoughts then glanced back at Prater. "I need you to promise to take care of Martha if I'm killed. I need you to promise me that you'll do it. Please. She'll be raising my sons alone. You aren't married, and it would be an honor to me."

Prater's eyes moistened as he stared into the eyes of his best friend and considered the reality that one of them might be killed within a few days. Would this be the last meal that he had with his best friend?

Prater accepted the bread that Brown passed to him. The reality of war was upon them. "I'm honored by your request. I pray that we both come home, but I will promise to take care of your family if something happens to you. You have my word." Prater stood up and Brown joined him in front of the campfire as the two men embraced. Tears moistened the eyes of the best friends. Then Brown pulled back and looked Prater in the eyes. His hands were now clasped together as if he was about to pray. "Thank you. Thank you, my friend."

Brown's mind quickly snapped back to the present as he felt his hands being bound with a leather strap. The leather stung as it was tightened around his wrists almost cutting off the circulation. Two men hoisted him to his feet and shoved him forward forcing him to walk down the hill where he would join over 5,000 other Confederates now destined for Rock Island, Illinois.

Chapter 2

Thomas Jefferson Brown climbed into the railcar as the other prisoners waited to board. Although the train was destined for the three mile long Mississippi River Island known as Rock Island, Illinois, it would take several days to arrive as a few hundred at a time poured into the camp. And by January 9th, 1864, just a few weeks after the Union victory at Missionary Ridge, all 6,158 captured Confederates had arrived.

L. Sydney Fisher

The prison camp had already been notified to expect an influx of prisoners from the battle at Missionary Ridge. On November 24, just one day before the battle, a guard assigned at the prison reported that he had "no blankets, no record book, no water in the prison yard, or clothing of any kind for the Confederates". And yet the prisoners were still boarded into the railcars and transported to what would become for many, their final destination.

Brown sat cramped in the middle of dozens of other soldiers piled almost on top of each other in the railcar. Although the conditions were not comfortable, the dozens of men cramped together generated enough body heat to help alleviate some of the bitter cold that seeped through the cracks in the railcar's door. And as the train traveled farther north crossing Indiana and much of Illinois, the train's lonely whistle faded into the sound of the howling wind as it slapped against the outside railcar's wall.

Brown's stomach churned and ached from lack of food, and he was becoming dehydrated. The cut above his left brow had finally ceased bleeding, but the stinging pain lingered as tiny pebbles of dirt and rock covered the open wound.

His mind drifted back to the battlefield. He remembered seeing the coattail of General Braxton Bragg at a distance as he narrowly escaped capture and certain death. The general's 5'10" slender frame faded into the background of his army's dead or captured men that now scattered the landscape. Brown remembered the general overseeing the camps in Tupelo, the headquarters of the Confederate Army of the West where he had spent the last several months before the day arrived when Bragg sent word to

General Manigault that his brigade would be departing by train the following day for Chattanooga, Tennessee. He now longed to feel the warmth of his wife's touch, but his heart had known since the day he left Alabama that he might never see those comforts again, and Tupelo might become the only remaining semblance of home.

Hours turned into days as the train passed through depots heavily lined with young recruits waiting to replenish the Union army. The men's morale hit an all-time low as the reality of their demise became certain. The "Cause" was undoubtedly hopeless as they contemplated a war that never seemed to end.

The train's wheels squealed against the steel rails as it came to a halt near the prison camp. The heavy steel doors slid open exposing daylight and mounds of glittering white powder that reflected the sun's light against a backdrop of ice laden trees. The men's eyes were squinted as they emptied the boxcar falling into snow two feet deep.

Brown struggled to put one foot in front of the other as he started the fourth of a mile trek toward the prison camp. Of the four hundred plus men that arrived with him, dozens of them found themselves barefoot in knee deep snow and fighting temperatures unlike anything they had ever experienced in the South's steamy climate. It was a different kind of hell. A hell where freezing to death or suffering frostbite to the feet was a common occurrence. With no blankets or clothing for Confederate soldiers who were already thinly clad, there was little hope for survival.

Brown finally reached the barracks that typically held 120 men with three tiers of bunks. With the temperature registering just above freezing at 35 degrees Fahrenheit, Brown was shivering so violently that he could barely stand on two feet. He stumbled inside the building hardly equipped to house hundreds of soldiers. The roof was all that was separating the men from the night skies and the falling snow. There was no ceiling and little protection against the elements other than the walls that blocked the icy, cold wind gusts that swirled and howled outside.

Brown followed the line of men until he reached the bunk now designated for him. He fell against the bed and curled into a ball as dozens of his Confederate friends did the same.

Within minutes, exhaustion overtook his body and his eyes closed.

By morning, Thomas Jefferson Brown joined the ranks of those who died within the walls of Rock Island, Illinois prison. Cause of death, exposure. His body lay motionless and hard as a block of ice. His fingers were unable to be pried open from the balled up fists that he held onto as his hands turned blue and slowly froze solid. The gash on his eye was no longer an open cut, but rather icy and sealed shut with traces of dried blood that had trickled down the side of his left cheek. Thomas Jefferson Brown would not suffer. His end had come fast, unlike many of the others who would spend months fighting disease and freezing temperatures.

Days later, Prater received word of his best friend's death making him the benefactor of Thomas Jefferson Brown's family, just as he had promised. While Brown's death was tragic, it was this destiny that was paving the way for a boy to be born four years later on April 21st, 1867 in Coosa County, Alabama. Because of his commitment to Thomas Jefferson Brown, Lewis Prater would father a child who would become a man destined to leave behind a legacy and a gift that only God could understand and the Devil could seek to destroy.

Chapter 3

The Gordon Hotel
January, 1880
Aberdeen, Mississippi

Seymour Prater stood outside the majestic red brick hotel located on East Commerce Street in Aberdeen, Mississippi. It had been years since Lewis Prater had married his best friend's widow and fathered a child with her. The couple lived a few years in Alabama after the War of the States ended and during Reconstruction. They then moved to Monroe County, Mississippi where the roots of Seymour Prater's supernatural legacy would be planted.

The small southern town of Aberdeen was located on the banks of the Tombigbee River where explorer Hernando De Soto had once camped. It had survived the Civil War with most of its buildings still intact, and the town now boasted a population of over 2,300 people.

Seymour gazed up at the second floor of the hotel admiring its grandeur. It was the finest hotel along the Tombigbee River Banks in North Mississippi. And it served the area well since Aberdeen was one of Mississippi's busiest ports in the land where cotton was king.

He put one foot onto the front walkway leading into the hotel and stopped. He quickly leaned back just in time to avoid being hit in the face as the door swung open. Patrons of the hotel, one right after another, followed past the open door to the horses and buggies that lined the front outside entrance. Seymour watched as three then five men dressed in charcoal gray, pinstripe suits and matching top hats exited the hotel. As the last man stepped forward through the doorway, Seymour rushed inside letting the door swing back against him.

John Davenport, Captain of the Tombigbee River boat *Johnson*, stepped inside The Gordon Hotel for the first time since its opening day. The interior first floor was bustling with shoppers and patrons visiting the hotel for a haircut in the barbershop or for browsing in the various merchant shops where they might purchase a fine tailored gentlemen's suit or a handcrafted leather hat and matching shoes now affordable from their recent cotton trade. But Davenport's mood was heavy laden with doubt and anxiety as he mulled an uncertain future since preparing for his final voyage down the Tombigbee River. He had been enlisted to oversee the Hargrove's estate for the past few years transporting cotton when the river water levels allowed. Today, the riverboat was forced to dock overnight as the river's water level registered just below the ten feet depths that were considered safe for travel to Columbus, Mississippi. With overcast skies and heavy rain expected by nightfall, the trip would most likely become navigable by mid-morning.

Davenport lifted his hat and raked strands of hair away from his eyes. He pushed the hat back down fitting it against his head and stood still with one hand on his hip as he glanced around the giant open area of the first floor. His eyes circled the room as he admired the decorative grandeur. The hotel's front desk was lined with guests checking into the area's newest and finest lodging place along the upper Tombigbee River. Hundreds of passengers from the many Tombigbee Riverboats had already visited the hotel within weeks of its "Open for Business" announcement. The hotel had been made possible by investors with the promise of a prosperous future to its tenants. Among the many occupants were entrepreneurs such as grocers, clothing merchants, barbershops, and the local newspaper, The Aberdeen Weekly.

Davenport walked to a nearby sitting area decorated by fancy carved wooden chairs that were upholstered with plush, red velvet cushions. He sat down and examined his boots that were covered with dust from the nearby street. He was in the wrong place. The hotel and the likes of it were much too fancy for him and his blood. He was a riverboat captain who spent many of his years sleeping in a bunk hardly equipped to house his large, tall frame. He was used to uncomfortable conditions, and it was a life that he had become accustomed to. The scenic route along the flowing riverbanks was a pristine existence where raccoons played, deer roamed, and the occasional glimpse of a panther climbing a low lying tree branch caused a rapid heartbeat as it locked eyes with Davenport.

His heart was on the Tombigbee River, and the thought of this being his last trip for Mr. W. H. Hargrove caused him much grief since the railroad would now be the main means of transportation for Hargrove's cotton. Would his riverboat find more work possibly transporting other goods to the area or even as far south as Mobile?

The young Seymour Prater watched people come and go from a corner of the hotel lobby where he positioned himself away from the traffic and inquisitive eyes of the hotel staff. He was a quiet kid with a curious nature who rarely missed an opportunity to help someone or offer advice that seemed well beyond his youthful years. He had never understood his bizarre ability to "see" into the nature of others and even determine their destinies through mental pictures that played out in his mind. And he had never told anybody about his uncanny gift for fear of ridicule or disbelief. It was an oddity that he endured alone except when he "felt" the need to share an insight that could not be withheld within his good conscious.

Seymour watched through the storefront window as his mother shopped in one of the grocer markets inside the hotel. Martha Prater savored the smell of fresh bread as she quickly lifted it to her nose before placing it into her basket. She joined dozens of other women this morning eager to shop among the hotel's many venues, and she had allowed Seymour to accompany her to the hotel since she would most likely need his assistance to carry her bags.

An invisible prompt suddenly caused Seymour to look away and turn his eyes toward John Davenport sitting in a chair across the room. He studied the man's expression and the way his body leaned forward in the chair, not sitting all the way back. He watched as the man studied his own feet. He noticed him bend over and down as he wiped his first two fingers across the toe of his boot before examining the rug beneath his feet.

Seymour's uncanny gift of insight began to come alive at that moment as he received invisible messages of the man's thoughts. It was as if he was plugging into a radio frequency that only John Davenport could hear, yet Seymour was an unknown invader who, regardless of his harmless intent, could no more control his own inclinations to see into the lives of another than he could control his body's natural urges of hunger or excretion.

Davenport's anxiety was real. He thought about the possibility of the railroad now taking over as a main means of transport. He knew that his security had been threatened. And while Davenport's thoughts filled the rafters of his mind, Seymour Prater listened in as the static became clearer. What would he do with the last two decades of his life now gone? He was a river captain, and John Davenport could not conceive of any other identity.

Seymour watched Davenport and sensed a need to address him. Flashes of insight in the form of pictures now flooded his mind. He became compelled to walk across the room and sit in the chair opposite and facing Davenport. Seymour ran his hands across the plush velvet seat of the chair feeling the soft texture and admiring the way the scarlet color seemed to change as he brushed his fingers back and forth.

Davenport glanced over at the young man sitting across from him and watched him with the same curiosity that had led Seymour across the room. What had brought the kid into the hotel lobby? Was he a runaway? Davenport studied the youth's demeanor for a few seconds before greeting him.

Davenport nodded and spoke in an even, friendly tone. "Good morning, young man. What brings you to this fine hotel?"

The corners of Seymour's mouth turned upward into a friendly smile. "Good Morning, Sir. This is my first visit to the hotel since it opened. I'm just waiting here for my mama while she shops." Seymour pointed toward one of the hotel storefronts.

"Ah, ok." Davenport nodded.

"You're a river captain, aren't you?" Seymour's inquisitive nature took over, relinquishing his otherwise shy disposition.

Davenport watched the boy's face. There was something odd about him in an uncanny kind of way. He looked to be about eleven years old, but his mannerisms, like the way he rubbed his eyes when he talked and the way he turned his head before he spoke, echoed the body language of someone much older. Like an elderly man. Yes, he reminded Davenport of an old man.

"Yes, I am. I've been a river boat captain—

"For over twenty years. Your home is on the river." Seymour interrupted, finishing his sentence. He paused and then continued to disclose glimpses of the mental images he had witnessed a few moments earlier.

"I saw you on the riverboat *Johnson*. You work for Mr. Hargrove, but you're scared that you won't have a job in a few months when he starts using the railroad. Don't worry." Seymour paused as Davenport stared in disbelief.

"Who are you, Kid? How do you know this?" Davenport leaned back in his seat and took a deep breath.

"I'm nobody, Sir. I just have some sort of odd talent, I guess." Seymour looked away and studied his hands folded in his lap.

"What do you mean that you 'saw me on the riverboat Johnson'?" Davenport was quickly forming an opinion about the boy, but he had questions of his own to ask.

"Oh, I just meant that I saw you in my mind. That's all." Seymour rubbed his fingers across his brow.

"You saw me in your mind? Can you see other things?" Davenport was now intrigued. He was well aware of Seymour's rare natural talent. He had only known one other person in his lifetime with the 'gift', but the former slave girl who lived on the Hargrove Plantation had been dead for years. Before being stricken with Typhoid Fever, she was considered to be Hargrove's most prized possession and often advised Master Hargrove of unseen troubles on the horizon. He had witnessed the supernatural wonders of her insights many times, and she had confided her secrets in Hargrove and Davenport who was often by his side more than anyone else in his circle. Davenport knew how she kept her abilities sharp. He knew what she was doing each morning before sunrise when she left the cabin and walked twenty feet to the old tree stump overshadowed by hanging vine and honeysuckle blooms. He had seen her sitting there with her eyes closed, not saying a word. Just still and quiet for several minutes until it was time to return to the morning's work at the plantation mansion.

"Yes, Sir. I see pictures. Not all the time, but I started seeing pictures about you almost as soon as you entered the hotel. And I knew that I should tell you not to worry." Seymour spoke barely above a whisper as people passed near them on their way to the hotel's front check-in counter.

Davenport sighed with relief and lifted his hat as he combed his hair back once again before standing to leave the hotel. He looked at the youth now standing before him in the hotel lobby. Seymour Prater had given him an important and timely message. He had offered encouragement and hope. And now Davenport knew that he must instruct Seymour Prater about the reality of his visions. He must instruct him to develop his abilities.

"What's your name, Kid?" Davenport reached out and patted Seymour on the shoulder.

"Seymour. Seymour Prater, Sir."

"Well, my good man, Seymour, it wasn't an accident that our paths crossed today. You understand that, don't you?" Davenport looked hard and straight in Seymour's eyes.

"Yes, Sir. I believe so."

"Good. Then here's what you need to do from this day forward and for the rest of your life. You must develop this special gift that you have. It will be your calling in life. You understand?"

Seymour nodded. "Yes, but I don't know how."

Davenport motioned for Seymour to step aside as hotel guests began to take the now empty seats that they had vacated. They took a few steps forward and stopped near the hotel's front door.

Davenport spoke clearly. "You must learn how to clear your mind and focus, Young Man. It's called meditation. You must practice this every day for a few minutes. It will open channels to you. First, find a quiet place to be alone and focus on a question in your mind, then be quiet and wait."

Seymour nodded in spite of the slight bit of confusion that he was feeling. He repeated Davenport's instructions. "Focus and clear my mind."

"Yes, that's right. I've only known one other person who could do it. And you will get better at it as time goes by. Now I have to get going. You do what I told you." Davenport patted Seymour once again on the back and reached for the door handle.

Seymour stood still in the doorway as he paused and watched John Davenport walk out ahead of him. Davenport looked back over his shoulder one last time and nodded as he spoke. "Focus. Good luck, young man." He turned the corner at the north end of the hotel and faded out of sight.

It would be the first and last time that Seymour ever saw John Davenport, but this chance meeting and Davenport's instructions would prove to be the most important guidance that he would ever receive. Davenport's timely message had set the stage for the beginning of what would become a supernatural legacy destined to be delivered by none other than Seymour R. Prater.

Chapter 4

January 3, 1931.
Deep in the Mississippi Delta of
Carrollton, Mississippi.
10:50 p.m.

Arthur Floyd reached inside the glass candy dish and grabbed a round piece of Peppermint candy. He placed the silver lid back on the jar as the metal tapped against the glass and clinked shut. A flicker of light entered his peripheral vision as it danced up and down the wall beside him. He turned and looked down the aisle toward the front door of the country store that he had owned and operated for the past ten years. A light bulb hung from an electrical cable near the front door of the store, but it was now swinging back and forth as if someone had pushed it. He studied the fixture and glanced around the displays of flour sacks and wooden crates located beneath the light. No one was visible to his eyes, but his ears weren't capable of alerting him of any danger since he had been born deaf and had spent all of his life in a world of silence.

Mr. Floyd mumbled thoughts of confusion and anxiety as he started toward the front of the room. His eyes were wide as he scanned the aisles from right to left, looking for the source that caused the swinging light fixture. He moved slowly toward the front door, his eyes now fixed on the lock that he had intended to secure. He wasn't aware of the occasional pop that his joints were making as he slowly walked forward. At 56 years old, Arthur Floyd suffered from chronic arthritis in his legs and hips. Although he was of average height at 5'9" and average weight of 159 pounds, he moved with a speed about the same as a turtle.

Arthur stopped and stood under the light fixture. Something didn't feel right. The front door was closed, and it appeared that he was the only person in the store. Yet someone sat crouched near the endcap where Arthur Floyd stood. Watching and waiting for just the right moment. The whites of his eyes were laced with a trail of bloody veins in the background of the deep, dark brown iris that matched the color of his skin.

The intruder grasped the handle of the ax tighter until the skin on his knuckles paled in color. He listened to Arthur's footsteps on the wide wood plank floor and the crackling and popping of Arthur's joints. He was just seconds away from the ambush that he and his brother were now about to execute.

Arthur paused and reached over his head to grab the swinging light. Just as his hand closed around the cable and the swinging ceased, the blunt force of an ax landed in the back of Arthur Floyd's head, not once, but twice. Powerful and fast.

One last guttural sound escaped from his lips as his hand dropped from the cable and his body collapsed to the floor with a hard and loud thud. Blood splatters covered the flour sacks and the front glass window while a pool of the bright crimson life force formed around his face branching off into small canals that oozed from the source of its flow. Arthur Floyd's demise was an immediate death with no warning other than the swinging light fixture that had alerted him of someone's presence.

The intruder rushed to Arthur's side and reached in his left side pants pocket digging for the keys to the store's office where Arthur kept operating cash and customer account records. He jerked out a large wad of keys attached to a metal ring then stood and reached for the front door as his brother turned the doorknob and pushed the front door open. He entered the store and stepped around Arthur Floyd's body. The murderer who had delivered the fatal blows reached for the lock and secured the door.

"You got the keys?" He whispered aloud.

The killer nodded and motioned for his brother to follow as he raced toward the back of the store and the office area. He quickly tried several keys before finding a match then pushed the door open and without wasting a fraction of a second, the two brothers emptied the safe, Arthur's desk, and the nearby book casings of any valuables that might be useful.

The murderer hurriedly walked to the corner of the door and glanced out into the store one last time before making his escape. His eyes focused on the dead man's body lying face down in the middle of the aisle near the front of the store, his left arm bent backwards and his palm closed still clutching the round piece of peppermint candy that he had pulled from the candy jar just moments before.

As the killer turned to walk out the back door, he remembered the weapon and ran to retrieve the ax now lying beside the corpse's head. He reached down and grabbed the handle clutching it as tightly as he had when he delivered the fatal blow that killed Arthur Floyd. As he stood back up, the killer's head tapped the lightbulb hanging from the cable. Startled by the touch and his fear of being caught inside the store with the dead body, the killer gasped and dropped the murder weapon onto the floor. He then made a fast retreat to the backdoor exit. As the door slammed behind him, a deafening silence filled the room with only the sound of the swinging electrical cable and its metal chain clinking against the lightbulb.

Swinging back and forth. Back and forth.

Clink. Clink. Clink.

A deaf man lay dead at the hands of two brothers who he had known. They had owed Arthur money. Money for goods that his generosity had allowed them. As Arthur Floyd lay dead, his eyelids were fixed and wide open with a stare that could only predict the haunting to come and a dead man's desire for revenge.

L. Sydney Fisher

———◆———

At just before dawn the following morning, the killer awakened, grabbed his coat off the back of a chair, and hurried out the door. He must return to the scene of the crime one final time. He had left the murder weapon and keys lying in the floor, but he had to get rid of it. He couldn't allow himself to get spooked again. He would do it fast. If he got there before the sun came up, he could get rid of it, and he knew where he could hide it. In the cistern at the bottom of the stairs leading to the basement. He had been down there once when he had helped Arthur Floyd carry some tools for storage. It was the perfect hiding place. The cistern in the basement stayed dry most of the time, and the killer reasoned that no one really knew that it was there since it wasn't being used anymore.

He hurried down the path that led to the Walton Farm. As he neared the rear entrance to Arthur's store, he could see the hanging light bulb that still illuminated the front of the store. He stepped onto the back porch steps and climbed to the top. The back door was still slightly ajar.

His breathing became heavy as he neared the opening to the store. The fear of being caught began to creep over him once again as he pushed the door open and rushed up the center aisle where the dead body of Arthur Floyd lay decaying. With wide eyes, the killer looked straight ahead at the front windows where blood had splattered across the glass. He then glanced down at the floor and searched for the ax and keys that he had dropped a few hours before. His eyes quickly landed on the murder weapon lying next to Arthur's right hand. The killer reached down, grabbed the keys and ax, and ran toward Arthur's office where the door leading to the basement was located.

He flung the door open and searched for a light, running his hand along the right side of the wall. His fingers found the wall socket and switched it to on as he skipped two steps at a time down the basement stairs. He reached the bottom of the stairs and swiftly walked to the cistern where he uncapped the covered hole by removing the wood board that had sealed it shut.

He pushed the board aside creating an opening and tossed the keys and ax to the bottom. The ax tapped the side of the metal receptacle and echoed as it hit a tiny puddle of water settled on the cistern's floor. The killer then pushed the wood cover back in place and raced back up the stairs, flicking off the light, and slamming the door behind him.

As he sprinted across the floor toward the exit, his eyes caught a glimpse of a shadow lurking up the wall beside him. Its form took the shape of a human body as it moved away from the wall. The killer jerked around. His pale blue eyes were bloodshot and watery as he stared at a strange black shadow that seemed to be suspended in air near the center aisle of the store. And then it vanished right before his eyes. Just as quickly as it had entered his peripheral vision, it was gone.

A freezing chill swept over the guilty man's body as he backed one foot at a time away from the center aisle and out the back door. With a sudden and uncanny awareness, the killer sensed the magnitude of his sin and the consequences that were coming.

Chapter 5

Monday morning, January 5, 1931

At just past sunrise, Phoebe Jones made her way along the familiar path to Arthur Floyd's store, limping on her bad foot from time to time. Although years had passed since the accident when she was trampled by a horse gone wild, she still had pain from where the bones in her foot had been shattered and had not grown back correctly.

See No Evil

The morning sun was bright and warming, but the cold January air still chilled her arms in spite of the wool wrap that covered her. Dust covered her shoes as she walked the dirt path located just beyond the wood shack she called home. As she neared the edge of the trees, she noticed the light bulb dangling from its cord, illuminating the inside of the store now just a few steps away.

Phoebe walked around the side of the building toward the front porch. She stepped onto the bottom wood step and began to climb the stairs when she noticed blood splatters covering the front window. Her face screwed up into a frightened stare as she inched closer toward the front door. She slowly walked to the window and leaned forward. She peered in and looked up and down the aisles. Then she let her eyes shift to both sides of the door. Nothing. But in a split second as she lowered her gaze to the floor, her body froze and her eyes became fixed on the sight before her. The dead and decaying corpse of Arthur Floyd was still lying face down in the same position where he had fallen two nights before. The gaping hole in his head was clearly visible, exposing brain matter in the busted, split skull.

Phoebe gasped as her hand immediately covered her mouth and tears spilled over her eyelids. She mouthed words of horror, shaking her head back and forth and slowly moving away from the door. Her feet were clumsy causing her to stumble off the porch and down the stairs, but she managed to regain her footing. Without looking back, she made a swift dash toward the sheriff's office at the end of the street.

Sheriff Frank Baker, a short and stocky man in his late 40's, sat in a wood swivel chair with his legs propped up on the corner of the desk as he read The Conservative. Although the newspaper's headquarters was located in the city of Winona about ten miles away, The Conservative covered the Carrollton area and any news events that happened there. It was Carrollton's link to the surrounding counties in Mississippi. If it happened in Carrollton, it was up to The Conservative to report it. Otherwise, no one would ever know.

Sheriff Baker heard screams coming from outside the office door. He jerked his legs down off the desk and looked out the front window where he saw Phoebe running straight toward his office, her eyes filled with tears and a terrifying fright that he had never seen in her before today. He rushed around his desk and flung the door open.

"What? What is it, Ms. Phoebe?" The sheriff asked in a southern drawl heard only in the deepest recesses of the American South.

"It's Mr. Floyd. He's dead. There's blood everywhere, Sheriff. Blood everywhere, I tell you!" Phoebe gasped, her breath forming a cold fog with each word that escaped her lips. She wiped an invisible sweat from her face that she imagined to be there, but her cheeks were only moistened by the tears that had seeped from her eyelids as she became the first witness of Arthur Floyd's murdered body.

The sheriff grabbed his hat off the corner of his desk and placed it on his head as he slammed the door behind him and motioned for Phoebe to follow him back to the store. He raced up the front steps and reached for the door handle. He turned the knob and pushed the door to no avail. It was still locked. He leaned forward and peered through the front window. Blood puddles still pooled around Arthur Floyd's head due to the cold January temperatures that delayed the decaying process and helped preserve the crime scene. With temperatures near freezing, rigor mortis and the putrefaction of tissues had been slowed.

The sheriff turned and started down the steps then turned back to face Phoebe who was reluctant to go any further toward the front door. He noticed the morbid stare in her eyes.

"Phoebe, go fetch Deputy Phillips, and tell him we have a body." Sheriff Baker's tone was somber. He paused as Phoebe stared back.

"Go. I'll get in the store somehow." The sheriff jumped off the top step to the ground and began to walk toward the back of the store.

"Yes Sir." Phoebe struggled to ease her trembling hands as she rubbed them together.

She then rushed past the sheriff and onto the same path that had brought her here.

Deputy Phillips lived about a ten minute walk away from the town's main street. He was the sheriff's right hand man and the town's local funeral director. It would be up to Phillips to transport the body of Arthur Floyd, deliver the news to Arthur's family, and arrange the burial after the investigation.

As Phoebe found herself at the deputy's house, she hurried across the front yard, climbed the two porch steps, and rapped on the screen door.

"Mr. Phillips! Mr. Phillips! The sheriff needs you!" Phoebe shouted with urgency.

A brief moment passed before the deputy appeared. Before he could ask any questions, Phoebe informed him of the morning's event.

"Mr. Floyd is dead. He's dead in his store. You've got to come now." The reality of her words sank in deep as Phoebe wrapped the cotton shawl tighter against her arms.

Deputy Phillips grabbed a coat and hat from the wall leaving his wife still sleeping in the comforts of their bed. He and his bride had been married twenty years, and she rarely missed a day of preparing breakfast for the deputy, but this morning, he quietly walked out the door and followed Phoebe across the front yard. As they both neared the path, he began asking questions.

"Where is the sheriff now?"

"He's at the store. He can't get in the front door. It's locked. He's gonna try to get in the back, but he told me to come get you." Phoebe explained.

"I see. Wait just a minute." He turned around and ran back toward the house with

Phoebe following close behind. As he flung open the door, he grabbed a set of keys hanging on the inside wall.

"Come on. Get in on the other side." The deputy noticed the fear that consumed Phoebe as her hands trembled while reaching for the door handle.

Phoebe climbed inside the town coroner's car and chewed her fingernails. She hoped that she could get back to the Walton Farm where she was the family's main housekeeper and cook. Her morning trip was only meant to purchase flour and a few other staples necessary for baking, and if she didn't return soon, the Walton's would be looking for her.

Deputy Phillips turned onto Main Street and drove the car to the front of the store. He stopped and pushed the gear shift into park as he reached for the door handle and turned the key in the car's ignition to off. He leaned over the back of the seat and grabbed a small black trunk that contained a camera and a few other items he would need at the scene. He then quickly pushed the door open and got out as he surveyed the area.

The deputy saw the sheriff standing inside the store and headed for the steps. Sheriff Baker motioned for him to stop. He lifted his hat off his head and placed it on top of a rack of canned goods. The sheriff then ran his fingers across his thin, graying hair and released a heavy sigh. He raised his arm and motioned with his thumb over his shoulder.

"Go around to the back. There's blood all over the place on the other side of that door!" The sheriff's voice was loud and clear.

Deputy Phillips turned; his 6'2" frame enabled him to take long strides as he rushed to the back of the brick building and jumped onto the back porch. He darted through the door and up the aisle to join the sheriff now standing over Arthur Floyd's corpse.

Although the cold temperature inside the store had delayed the decaying process, it was apparent to Phillips that the body had been dead for more than 24 hours. The town coroner slowly bent down resting his knees on the floor while sitting against his ankles as he examined the gaping wound on the back of Arthur Floyd's skull. He pulled a tape measure from his pocket and held it over the victim's head without touching the body. He noticed the purple-red skin discoloration on Arthur's face, neck, and hands. And Arthur's eyes remained open and fixed with the eyelids frozen in place.

The fatal injury measured approximately four inches along the middle left area of the skull.

Phillips analyzed the slit and determined that the weapon was administered with a blunt force so powerful that it left broken bits of the victim's cranium within the gray and black hair now stained with dry blood. Phillips stood up and removed a camera from the trunk that he had set next to the center aisle. He began snapping pictures while the sheriff recorded details of the scene on a small notepad he carried in his shirt pocket.

"Who could do this to Arthur?" Deputy Phillips asked as he moved around the body photographing the scene at different angles. "Somebody wanted him dead quick. Whoever did this hit him more than once. You see any weapons lying around?"

The sheriff shook his head. "Nothing, but look at his left hand. There's a piece of candy folded inside his hand. Looks like he was caught by surprise. Somebody was waiting for him right here."

A distant memory suddenly flashed through the sheriff's mind. He remembered the last dead body that he had looked upon, and he remembered the displeasure of having to notify the next of kin. It was a part of the job that he disliked the most, but a fifteen year career in law enforcement had made Baker a thankful man for the devoted woman and son he had at home. He believed in living by the law and executing the proper punishments for those who broke the law, but he was a kind man behind the tough exterior and rugged ways. For those who had known Baker all his life, he was just a stern man with a deep, harsh voice that softened like butter in the presence of his wife.

The deputy looked at Baker with raised eyebrows. "A robbery?" He scratched his brow and wiped his nose with a handkerchief he pulled from his back pants pocket.

"Yeah, looks like they went through Arthur's desk." The sheriff shook his head as he looked down at Mr. Floyd's dead body. The whole town would be affected by the killing. Everyone was a neighbor to each other in this small community known as Carrollton. The Mississippi Delta town was located on the south side of Big Sand Creek with a population of approximately five hundred twenty people. Half of those people were black and the other half white. Most everyone got along well with little or no crime to speak of until now.

The deputy looked at the sheriff and pointed toward Phoebe who stood at the backdoor of the store. "What does she know?"

The sheriff shook his head. "Don't know yet. She came running to my office just a few minutes ago. She found the body."

"But she didn't enter the store, did she?" The deputy asked.

"Not that I know of." The sheriff looked at Phoebe who refused to step any further than the back door entrance.

"Ms. Phoebe?" The deputy called out.

Phoebe peered around a display case blocking her view of the deputy. "Yes, Sir?"

"I need you to stay right there for a few minutes. I'm gonna need to ask you a few questions." The deputy watched her.

Phoebe nodded then objected. "Yes, Sir, but Mrs. Walton gonna come looking for me in a minute, Sir."

The sheriff looked at Phillips and nodded indicating that he would take care of Phoebe while the deputy prepared to remove the body.

The sheriff walked to the back of the store and faced Phoebe. "Ms. Phoebe, were you the only one here when you found Mr. Floyd?"

"Yes, Sir." Phoebe's eyes watered.

"Where were you when you found him?"

"I was standing on the front porch, Sir. I saw him through the front door."

"What did you do next?" The sheriff studied her.

"I started crying and ran to get you!" Phoebe's eyes moistened again.

"And you didn't see anybody else around here? Nobody walking past the store or anything else going on?"

Phoebe shook her head with her eyes closed and her face screwed up in a grievous expression.

The sheriff nodded and took a deep breath. "Ok, you can go on home now."

Phoebe backed out the door without turning around. Images of Arthur Floyd's face left an imprint in her mind as she struggled to erase the memory, but it haunted her. They were horrific images that warned her of the coming resurrection of a murdered man. She had looked into the eyes of Arthur Floyd. A dead man with a soul now doomed to be a wandering ghost, and although she had not touched the corpse or any of his belongings, she felt unclean.

Yes, she must get back to the Walton Farm and her home as soon as possible. She had to tell everyone who would listen. Arthur Floyd had been murdered in cold blood, and his ghost

See No Evil

would surely seek revenge upon the town of Carrollton, Mississippi.

Chapter 6

  Sheriff Baker helped the deputy lift the cold body of Arthur Floyd and place it onto a long cotton sheet. The dead man's limbs were hard and inflexible making it difficult to secure them close to the side of the body. Members of the deputy's staff at the funeral home would be responsible for massaging the limbs into position so that the body could be prepared for burial.

After Phillips slammed the back door to the car, he turned and faced Baker. "You got any idea who would wanna do this to Arthur? Far as I know, he never hurt nobody."

The sheriff shook his head. "Don't know. But you can damn bet that I'm gonna do my best to find the guilty bastard and when I do, I'm gonna hang him." The look of determination on the sheriff's face left no questions about the intensity of his statement. Carrollton was a small town with a close knit group of people, but there was a killer now loose.

Unknown to Sheriff Baker, he was already being watched by guilty eyes and the killer wasn't about to take them off of the sheriff's investigation. With Arthur Floyd dead, the killer knew his fate would be sealed from the branch of an oak tree on the courthouse lawn.

The deputy nodded in agreement. "Makes no sense to me, but I'm gonna say that Arthur has been laying in the front of that store since Saturday night 'cause I saw him through the front window as I passed by on my way home."

"What time was it? You remember?" The sheriff inquired.

"Yeah, it was about 9:00 that evening." The deputy said.

The sheriff stared off into the distance, his lips pursed together as he contemplated who committed the murder and how they did it. "But doesn't Arthur close the store about 5:00?"

Deputy Phillips nodded. "Yeah, I believe that's right." He paused for a second, then raised his finger in the air and spoke with confidence. "Well, then that might mean he knew his killer."

"Could have. The front door was locked. The back door was open. And the light was still on. Looks like Arthur walked to the front when someone surprised him from behind." Sheriff Baker reasoned.

"I say we start questioning everybody we can find who visited that store on Saturday. We've got to break the news to Arthur's family first. I'll go over to Bobby's if you don't mind telling William."

"That's his only kin folk? Just his brothers?" The deputy asked.

"Far as I know." Sheriff Baker confirmed.

The deputy opened the car door and got in. He cranked the car and began to back out of the drive when the sheriff motioned for him to roll down the window.

"I'm going to see Bobby now, but let's meet here tomorrow morning at dawn. You know Ms. Phoebe is going to be spreading this news like wildfire if she hasn't already, and I don't want anybody leaving town." Sheriff Baker's tone was stern. He raised his hand in a final wave as Phillips shifted the car into reverse.

As the sun was rising the following morning, Sheriff Baker and Deputy Phillips began their questioning of the local townsfolk. Without a murder weapon, the sheriff had little or nothing to go on.

As expected, Bobby and William Floyd didn't take the news of Arthur's death well. After several minutes of grieving for the brother they both claimed as "just a gentle deaf man who loved everybody", they vowed to find his killers and deliver justice to his killer even if it meant being the executioner. And the town wasn't safe any longer. Someone who murdered an innocent, unarmed man was still on the loose. Would they kill again? The murderers had butchered Arthur Floyd with the blade of an ax so sharp that it had almost severed his skull in half. Who would have done such a heinous act?

Phoebe Jones raced to tell her story to anyone who would listen. She had looked into the eyes of Arthur Floyd, and she knew what was coming. His spirit would not rest. Not a minute. His spirit was probably already roaming the floors of the store, watching and waiting for the killers to return to the scene of their crime. No, the ghost of Arthur Floyd would not rest until they were confronted.

Bobby and William Floyd were allowed to begin the cleanup of the store and take over the business. The sheriff and deputy had finished taking pictures of the scene and had no other investigation business to do there after sunrise the following morning. But the town's people had already begun to gather out front where they stood and stared in disbelief at the blood splatters on the front windows. As William scrubbed the red stains from the wood floor, dozens of people stood outside whispering about the horrific scene and the reality of a murderer still at large.

William kneeled on his hands and knees, scrubbing the scene where Arthur's body had laid. His arms began to ache and tire as he struggled to remove the red stains that seemed to reappear each time he rinsed the dirty rag in the water pail sitting beside him. The stains were not lifting from the wood floor in spite of how low the temperature had been inside the room over the past two days. Although the bloody mess was dry on the windows and in some places on the floor, it was still pooled where Arthur's head rested after the fall.

William Floyd began to feel sick at his stomach as nausea began to creep up into his throat. The scene was too much for him, and he began to cough and gag. His eyes watered and he struggled to stand up. He needed to get outside for fresh air.

Bobby looked around the corner of the door to Arthur's office where he had been cleaning up the broken and scattered debris from the killer's rampage. He saw William stumbling and rushed out the door toward the front of the store.

"William. William, what's wrong?" Bobby reached for his brother's arm and helped him out the door and onto the front porch as he gasped for air.

Phoebe was among the people still standing outside observing the scene when William almost fell onto the porch. Her mind immediately raced with thoughts of the haunting that was destined to become known in the community. How long would it be before the deceased's spirit came back to avenge his death? She must not cross the path of the blood stains or ever allow her feet to touch the spot where Arthur was murdered.

William sputtered and spit. "I can't do it. I can't finish that. I've cleaned that damn floor three times. The stain won't come up." William stood and shook his head as he wiped his mouth across the sleeve of his shirt. He was the exact likeness of his dead brother, except for the extra two inches in height that William had been blessed with, at 5'11" tall and weighing in at 170 pounds. And he and Arthur also shared the same large, distinctive nose that made them memorable.

Bobby's brow shifted into a worried frown as he stared at his brother, unable to comment. Then after a long pause, he offered a response that came as a relief to William. "You go to the back, and I'll finish this up."

William let out a sigh and nodded as he turned and reached for the doorknob. He pushed open the door and walked around the bucket of dirty, blood stained water while forcing his eyes to look straight ahead. He didn't dare look down at the spot where he had been vigorously scrubbing for the past twenty minutes. He was unnerved and sickened by thoughts of the murder. If his grief wasn't enough, he now had to clean up the site where his brother lay dead just hours ago, and the stubborn blood stains on the wood floor seemed to send a spine-tingling reminder that would be etched forever in the building's history. A living reminder that horrific acts can happen anywhere, even in the smallest and most seemingly safe cities.

 A cold gust of wind came swirling through the front door rushing past William as he walked toward the back of the store. The blast caught Bobby in the face causing his chestnut brown eyes to water and his body to jerk. He quickly reached for the door as the wind howled and swung it back and forth on its hinges in spite of the fact that there had not been any windy weather that morning. It seemed to come out of nowhere. Then just as Bobby placed his hand on the doorknob, the hanging light bulb that had dangled over Arthur Floyd's dead body exploded sending shards of glass in multiple directions while at the same moment, the door slammed violently shut. Screams came from the audience of onlookers standing outside the building. Just a split second later, the locks clicked into place right before everyone's eyes sending Phoebe and the others into a panic as they rushed down the street and away from the store.

The onlooker's curiosity that had summoned them to the store this morning was beyond what anyone was prepared for. No one had expected to witness the return of Arthur Floyd. No one except Phoebe. She had already told too many people about the dead man's eyes that had stared at her through the front door on the morning that she found the body. She told everyone about the curse of Arthur Floyd that was certain to haunt the town of Carrollton and anyone who entered the store.

Within 24 hours, Phoebe Jones had already implored the help of the African American congregation and had managed to spread the news of the "haunted Floyd place" to over one quarter of the town's population. Phoebe believed her ancient African practices and rituals would help the soul of Arthur Floyd as he transitioned into the afterlife, but she had no idea that she was entering a realm of hell where she was about to become one of the haunted.

Chapter 7

Phoebe wrestled against the images that drifted in and out of her consciousness as she lay sleeping against a pile of crumpled and worn quilts. A stack of burnt logs was all that remained for providing warmth in the shotgun cabin's tiny fireplace, the orange and red embers still glowing hours later. And the sound of silence surrounded her except for the occasional howling of a crisp, cold wind that bounced and slapped against the outside walls.

Phoebe whimpered in her sleep and rolled to the left facing the wall. She heard whispers. Even in the deepest slumber, Phoebe could hear the panicked whisper of a man desperately trying to reach her. His words were vague, but audible.

You know.

It came again. This time louder and more violent.

You know who killed me.

Phoebe stirred trying to get awake as the man appeared before her. At first, he was shadowed by darkness and then with what seemed like one swift movement, he was walking fast toward her. He was coming into the light, his face appearing out of the shadows. A faint guttural voice came again.

You know my killers.

But she didn't. She wasn't there when Arthur Floyd was murdered.

Phoebe stirred, desperate now to get awake. It was her only escape as the man took his final step toward a certain confrontation with her. Phoebe jerked and rolled over slinging a quilt out of the way. Her breathing was now heavy and panicked as she stared into an empty room. But wait! The shadow was there floating in mid-air. It began to materialize right before her eyes. His face was white with channels of veins that protruded from his skin against a background of bright crimson blood and empty eye sockets.

Phoebe's body trembled while her face became flooded by a river of fear. She screamed wails of terror that echoed throughout the cabin as she bolted past the ghost of Arthur Floyd who now stood before her mouthing the words *You Know.*

Meanwhile, William and Bobby Floyd were of no help to the sheriff as he and the deputy searched the store and the outside property for the third time hoping to find the murder weapon and the missing store keys that contained the only key to the vault. Whoever entered the store and killed Arthur Floyd must have discarded or hid the keys and the bloody hatchet, but the hopes of finding anything were growing slim as the hours turned into Day Three.

The sheriff and deputy had almost exhausted their short list of interviewees who had visited the store that day, and with the funeral now scheduled for mid-afternoon on Wednesday, the only thing left to do was post a reward for information that might lead to an arrest. William and Bobby conversed in the privacy of Arthur Floyd's office as they prepared to hang posters on every storefront in Carrollton, Mississippi.

Bobby searched the tool box next to Arthur's desk looking for a hammer and a few nails that were needed to hang the posters around town. He carried a bundle of ten signs, rolled up and secured with a rubber band by the printer in Greenwood that had delivered them to the store earlier in the day. The message was clear, and the money was guaranteed to be paid to anyone with information about the murder. A hanging was eminent with the guilty party promised a speedy execution.

REWARD

➡ $100

FOR INFORMATION IN THE ROBBERY AND MURDER OF ARTHUR FLOYD ON THE NIGHT OF JANUARY 3RD, 1931. ANY INFORMATION THAT LEADS TO AN ARREST AND CONVICTION WILL BE REWARDED UPON THE GUILTY'S EXECUTION OF HANGING BY THE NECK UNTIL HE IS DEAD.

JUSTICE FOR THE MURDER OF ARTHUR FLOYD

ON THE NIGHT OF SATURDAY, JANUARY 3RD, SOMEONE ENTERED ARTHUR FLOYD'S STORE AND KILLED HIM BY HITTING HIM IN THE HEAD WITH A WEAPON BELIEVED TO BE AN AX. HE WAS LEFT DEAD, FACE DOWN NEAR THE FRONT OF THE STORE. A PIECE OF PEPPERMINT CANDY WAS FOUND STILL CLASPED IN HIS HAND. ARTHUR MAY HAVE KNOWN HIS KILLER. IF YOU HAVE INFORMATION, CONTACT SHERIFF BAKER OR DEPUTY PHILLIPS IN CARROLLTON, MISSISSIPPI.

January 7, 1931

William Floyd was growing impatient with an intensity that made it hard to focus on anything else except finding his brother's killer. He began to realize that they needed something extraordinary to happen if they were ever going to find out what happened. There was absolutely no evidence to piece the puzzle together. If somebody knew who killed Arthur Floyd, they weren't talking. The case was growing cold quick in the small town, but the rumors of Arthur Floyd's vengeful spirit were spreading like a plague infecting the community with fear and dread.

As Phoebe proclaimed the haunting at the Floyd place, Bobby and William Floyd made plans to travel the two hour drive to Pontotoc, Mississippi where they would seek the help of a man believed to hold prophetic powers. The Mississippi Mystic, with a supernatural gift like the famous Edgar Cayce from Kentucky was about to unveil a killer in less than eight hours.

Chapter 8

Seymour Prater opened the screen door and walked out onto the front porch of his home in Pontotoc, Mississippi. His six feet, one inch slender frame glided to the corner of the porch where he stopped and looked as far to the left and right as he could see. His piercing blue eyes seemed to penetrate an invisible veil in the flat bottom land of Cooper's Crossing Road.

The flowing waters of Chiwapa Creek could be seen in the distance across from a grassy field where Seymour's mule and a few cattle roamed free. Small, lush green shrubbery and flowering trees lined the banks of the creek where the natives of the Chickasaw Nation had once fished and hunted wild game. Now the only remnants of their existence, was a treasure hunter's occasional find of a flint arrowhead or spearhead lying buried in the muddy creek.

Seymour stepped off the porch and walked toward the fence that surrounded the property. His uncanny ability to find lost objects was no good this morning. Although he was now renowned all across the South for being a modern day prophet of sorts, he couldn't solve his own mystery. Closing his eyes and summoning his inner powers was not working, but in reality the "gift" was rarely something that could be easily manipulated. He had never forgotten the encounter that he had as a young boy when he met Mr. Davenport at The Gordon Hotel in Aberdeen. Mr. Davenport had served as an important messenger in Seymour Prater's destiny and now years later, he was still practicing the mysterious art of clairvoyance and extra sensory perception, although most of the time he didn't understand exactly what his "gift" was or how it worked.

His ability was also characteristic of a man from Kentucky named Edgar Cayce, otherwise known as the Sleeping Prophet. Although the two men didn't know each other, Cayce's path had almost mirrored Seymour Prater's path as the two men shared ties to Alabama cities only seventy miles apart. And while Prater's messenger had been the sudden appearance of a man delivering a message to him in an Aberdeen hotel in 1880, Cayce's messenger appeared to him in the form of an angel during Cayce's youth, telling him that his "gift" could be accessed during sleep when he would be able to receive prophetic messages and healing cures never heard of or seen before.

Seymour's insights and predictions were correct ninety-nine percent of the time when people sought his assistance. Many were known to have traveled hundreds of miles in search of answers that lay hidden within the recesses of his supernatural power. He often referred to himself as "the man with the radio mind", a description that defined his ability to tune into an invisible channel that allowed him to see pictures behind closed eyes. As he massaged his temples and eyelids with his fingertips, he spoke aloud, delivering extraordinary messages to seekers.

The now sixty-four year old Seymour Prater lived a peaceful life in the rural town, a life steeped in southern culture and family values. After spending a few years in Texas working as a detective in local law enforcement, he returned to the area where his wife's roots run deep and where he could spend the remainder of his life as a farmer and plantationer.

Sundays were a time of worship and fellowship when families came together for the usual after church gatherings. Picnic tables were lined to capacity with southern delicacies such as fried okra and fresh vegetables straight out of the garden. Baskets filled with breads and cobblers could be found on all four corners while roasted chicken was often served as the meat of the day.

His life was nothing that he considered extraordinary, but rather a blessing from God. He was known to be a loving, generous, and kind man to members of the community who knew him. And although hundreds of people made the journey seeking his help, he refused to accept any monetary payment for his supernatural services. He was given a gift from God, and it was meant to be shared. It was meant to help people. Charging a fee would have compromised his principles. He was helping people find prized possessions that they had lost. Prized possessions that even included missing children and family members.

He had identified the culprit who had poisoned his neighbor's dog, not once but twice. And he had successfully revealed the perfect description of a robber unknown without the help of Seymour Prater. But he had never identified a man's killer. He had never relived the horror of a murder scene and felt the agonizing residual energy of the slain victim. Until now, Seymour had only used his extraordinary powers to uncover secrets among the living. And fate was about to have its way as the car being driven by William Floyd reached the front entrance to the Prater Farm.

William Floyd drove his 1925 Dodge Brothers sedan down the winding gravel road to the Prater Farm. Bobby sat quiet and contemplative in the passenger seat as his mind reeled with ideas about the killing. Neighbors and friends from as far as Jackson, Mississippi had recommended the Pontotoc man, Seymour Prater, as a prophet who could "see" things like a fortune teller. No one knew how he did it, but many were eager to share their stories and swore by his ability to solve mysteries. It was enough to persuade the brothers to make the trip.

Seymour Prater heard the sound of the car's engine percolating in the distance as it began to near the edge of the fence that surrounded the outside of the property. He glanced in the direction of the sound from the creek bank where he now stood and just minutes before had found his mule with its hoof mired down in the mud. He watched as William Floyd turned the car onto the rock driveway, then he gave the mule a nudge, leading him back in the direction of the house.

Seymour looked straight ahead and for a brief moment, he erased any thoughts wandering through his mind and instead focused solely on the two men traveling up the driveway. His crystal blue eyes moistened as a cold wind whipped across his face and a warm fog escaped his lips each time he breathed out. The path ahead seemed to blur as images began to flash before him, and it was unlike anything he had ever seen. A bloody death and a rotting corpse continued to flash on and off in Seymour's mind, causing him to shut his eyes in horror. Finding lost objects and identifying a guilty robber was one thing, but reliving a man's murder through a supernatural ability to see the past was something he wasn't prepared for.

William Floyd parked the car and got out with Bobby following close behind. Seymour exited the gate leading to the pasture and lifted his hand in the air with a wave to the two men now walking toward him.

"Good morning, Sir!" William Floyd called out to Seymour. "I hope me and my brother have reached the right place. Are you Mr. Prater, that prophet that we've heard of?"

William met Seymour before he reached the porch steps and extended his hand.

"Yes, sir. I am Seymour Prater." He accepted William's handshake with a firm grip and a friendly smile, but ignored the 'prophet' comment. "What brings you gentlemen here?"

"Our brother has been murdered in Carrollton. Whoever did this--- they almost chopped his head in half. And the sheriff?" William paused. "He ain't got no more leads to go on." He shook his head and squeezed his fists resting at his sides.

Bobby nodded in agreement then spoke to Seymour with certainty, his tone clear. "We don't know who did this, but we heard that you could help us."

Seymour nodded and looked at the men with sympathetic eyes. "Sometimes I can. You gentlemen come on up here on the porch and sit down."

The men followed him onto the porch and sat down on a wood bench across from Seymour's favorite chair. "Who was your brother?"

"Arthur Floyd. His name was Arthur Floyd, Sir." Bobby replied.

"Uh huh." Seymour responded with a slight tone of surprise and a nod, but just then a flash of insight crowded his mind. He saw the swinging light above Arthur's dead body. He flinched and shifted in his chair.

Seymour leaned forward and placed his fingertips against his eyelids, rubbing them back and forth. "I see- I see two people. They entered the store from the back. No, wait. One entered the store from the front and the other one waited at the rear of the building. Your brother never knew they were there."

Bobby and William sat quiet for a moment.

"Our brother was deaf. We found him at the front of the store." William interjected.

"Yes, but he was in the back when the first man came in. I see him. The two of them. They are brothers."

William froze, his body rigid, and his eyes fixed on Seymour Prater as he continued to describe the murder scene. Bobby leaned back against the wall as a strange sensation covered his body like a spider crawling across his skin. The two of them became mesmerized as they listened, not daring to interrupt or cause Seymour to lose focus.

Seymour continued, his eyes still closed, but his fingers now rested against his temples as he massaged the sides of his face in a circular motion. "They hid the murder weapon in the cistern. And the keys. The keys to the store are there too."

Bobby and William looked at each other then back at Seymour.

"The killers have dark skin. They are watching you and the sheriff. Who is Phoebe?"

William looked stunned. "Phoebe? Well- Ms. Phoebe is a Negro. She works for the Walton's. Why?"

Seymour hesitated and then opened his eyes. "Phoebe found the body."

"Yes, that's right." Bobby nodded as he spoke confirming Seymour's statement.

"She knows the killers." Seymour stated this with certainty.

"She knows who did this?" William jumped to his feet, his voice rising.

Seymour shook his head. "I can't declare that, but I believe that she knows the people who killed your brother."

Bobby stood and joined William now standing beside Seymour. "Well, we better get the sheriff to question that Negro again before the killers try to leave town."

Seymour locked eyes with William. "Be careful. The colored woman is innocent."

Bobby nodded. "I don't believe Ms. Phoebe had nothing to do with this, but if she knows something---

William stopped him. "Don't you know what Phoebe has been telling all those Negros? She's been telling them that 'the Floyd Place is haunted'. She's got the whole damn Negro community scared to death. The killers may already be gone."

Seymour shook his head. "No, they ain't gone. Have the sheriff question anyone meeting the description that I gave you."

"You can't give us a name?" Bobby implored.

Seymour was adamant with his response shaking his head as he spoke. "No. I don't know their names."

Bobby and William now realized this was the only information that they would get from Seymour Prater, but it was more than they had before they arrived. The two men extended their hands and gave a firm handshake as they said good-bye.

Seymour watched the men step down off the porch and walk back to their car. The men got in and slammed the doors shut. As the car traveled away from the house, Seymour saw the men's hands as they waved out the car window.

See No Evil

Just as the car's tires touched the road leading out of Pontotoc, Seymour Prater felt a gut-wrenching urge to vomit. He gagged and leaned forward, grabbing his stomach as he witnessed the final image of Arthur Floyd. The killers aimed the ax at his head and slammed it, not once, but twice as he fell to the floor. But the violent gags came faster as Seymour Prater now realized Phoebe's role in the murder of Arthur Floyd. And like Phoebe, he had become another living witness to the murder. A living witness with a supernatural ability to not only see events and times where he had not ever physically been, but also he became a conduit for the spirit of Arthur Floyd who would not rest until justice set his soul free.

L. Sydney Fisher

Chapter 9

Beads of sweat glistened across the dark, smooth skin of Phoebe's forehead as she stirred in the final ingredients that would complete the concoction she needed. While others were sleeping in the small town of Carrollton, Mississippi, she was preparing to hold a ritual at the gravesite of Arthur Floyd. She would attempt to make peace with the spirit who had visited her the day before. It absolutely must be done. His spirit had become trapped and confused. Phoebe was sure of it. The spirit of Arthur Floyd was tormenting her, and the torment would continue if she didn't intervene and cast his spirit away.

It was close to midnight, and Phoebe had to hurry. She quickly gathered a makeshift bag which was now just an empty flour sack and filled it with mustard seeds, ground garlic, leaves of sage, and a liquid concoction made from boiling the bulb of a daffodil.

She wrapped her shoulders with the same wool shawl she always wore and quietly pulled the door shut, careful not to wake the Walton's dog that slept a few feet away from her cabin's door. Phoebe's cabin was located at the Walton Farm, behind the main house where she worked and tended to the family. She knew she was a blessed woman to have a place provided for her even if it was only a two room shack. Times were hard. People were lucky to have food to eat and many didn't.

Phoebe's roots could be traced back to Charleston, South Carolina where her sixteen year-old great-grandmother arrived aboard the ship, Edgefield on April 22, 1820. She was Phoebe's namesake and the property of Colonel H.K. Hugan until she was sold and re-located to a cotton plantation in the Mississippi Delta where she lived until she died.

Phoebe's knowledge of herbs, their properties, and powers had been handed down over the past two generations. And like most other black folks in her community, the reality of death and dying wasn't taken lightly lest you find yourself with a flying spirit or a wandering ghost that was unable to adapt to life in the spiritual world, making it a danger to the living.

Phoebe knew the minute she witnessed the murdered body of Arthur Floyd that she was in danger of becoming haunted by his spirit. His eyes were open and fixed that day, and she had stared directly into them. Arthur's ghost must have believed that she knew his killer. Maybe his ghost believed that *she* was the killer. Either way, Phoebe had to protect herself and set the spirit of Arthur Floyd free from the binding throes of his fate.

Phoebe hurried through the darkness toward the city cemetery around the corner from Arthur's store. The red clay dirt was still fresh and powdery dry from the burial of his body just days before. Because it had not rained in Carrollton since the funeral, the dirt would be easy to scoop with her hands.

Phoebe neared the front gates to the cemetery. A misty fog drifted above a few dozen tombstones illuminated by the bright full moon that seemed to be suspended over the cemetery as if it was hanging from an invisible anchor above her head. She crossed under the gate's arch and carefully crept around the side of the graves until she reached the fresh mound of clay that indicated the site of Arthur Floyd's grave. The sound of an animal scurrying across dry, fallen leaves startled her as she laid her materials on the ground. She jerked around and saw nothing. Then she quickly lit a candle and held it firmly in her hand.

  Phoebe needed to work fast. She had already encountered the ghost of Arthur Floyd, and she had put herself in danger by coming here. Her mere presence at the dead man's grave could irritate his soul even more if the ritual wasn't successful in banishing him from haunting her.

She spread the herbs on a cotton cloth then scooped a handful of the grave's dirt while she chanted a prayer to release the haunted curse. She began to sprinkle the herbs with the dirt in a circular motion around the four corners of the dead man's grave. Her voice was barely above a whisper but audible to anybody or *anything* nearby.

As Phoebe chanted and called out to Arthur Floyd, her feet began to feel lite and her body began to tremble. The night was without even an occasional zephyr, and the silence of the dead intensified Phoebe's anxiety. The creepy atmosphere sent chills crawling over her body, and then it came at once. The sudden urge to run. Phoebe looked up and all around. The candle's flame flickered and danced back and forth in the still air, but its motion appeared to be manipulated by something unseen. She froze dead still as she watched the flame of her candle bending over as if it was about to go out. Then she heard it. The sound of someone blowing out a candle. Heaving and panting in short, abrupt puffs.

Phoebe's heart began to race as she attempted to back away in haste, but just as she turned to toss the remainder of the herbs toward the center of the grave, she felt the cold, clammy fingertips of the dead against the skin on her neck. First, there was a moan. It came once then again as a growl that crescendoed into a screech that pierced Phoebe's ears. She screamed out in horror, her voice broken by tearful wails as she stumbled backwards and fell at the foot of Arthur Floyd's grave.

As Phoebe rolled over on her side scrambling to get up, her eyes caught the appearance of two red dots hovering directly in front of her.

The red dots were centered in the eye sockets of something sinister that had been watching her from a distance. It hissed again and moved closer. Phoebe screamed out, ordering the invisible predator away.

Its final growl came loud and fierce as she covered her face with her arm and jumped to her feet, racing across the cemetery to the main gate. She didn't bother to watch where she was stepping. Her lungs began to tire as she darted across the resting place of the dead, but she refused to stop until she saw the outer path that led down the hill, away from the town square and straight to her cabin.

Phoebe's chest ached as it rose and fell hard, her heart beating hard and fast. She jerked the door open and rushed inside, slamming it behind her as she fastened the lock. She was consumed by exhaustion and despair as she leaned back against the door and cried in anguish while a steady stream of warm tears bathed her cheeks. She lowered her head with her chin resting on her chest and rubbed sorrow from her eyes. She had been chased away from Arthur Floyd's grave by something, but *what?* Had his spirit been taken over by the "evil ones"?

Phoebe had no idea that anyone had followed her. Yet off in the distance, the old man who dug and prepared the graves for the town's deceased had seen her as she escaped the cemetery. He had heard her screams from his nearby shack, and he had come to the corner of the graveyard searching for the source of the sound only to see the tail of Phoebe's dress as she ran through the front gates.

Phoebe felt her face become flushed and her cheeks hot and feverish. She slowly moved toward her bed as she fought against the dizzy sensation that consumed her. As she placed her hand on the bedpost, she lowered her body across the bed and collapsed. Fatigue consumed her, and she fell into a deep sleep that would last for more than six hours until a knock at the cabin door awakened her.

Chapter 10

It was just past sunrise when Sheriff Baker and the Floyd brothers made their way to the Walton Farm. They knocked on the front door of the stately red brick home and questioned Frederick Walton about his hired hand, Phoebe Jones and her whereabouts over the past few days. Mr. Walton couldn't provide any details that the sheriff didn't already know, but he did seem concerned with the possibility that Phoebe was keeping secrets about Arthur Floyd's murder.

Rumors were now flying around the community since Phoebe had found the body and raced to the sheriff's office just days before. She had hoped to calm the unrest the night before when she visited Arthur's grave, but hours later, the Black community now gathered in the small neighborhood only blocks away from Arthur Floyd's store. Phoebe had unintentionally instilled fear into the neighborhood where many of her family and friends lived. A town that was known for its peace and community spirit was now being terrorized by the rumored haunting of Arthur Floyd.

Everyone feared being a suspect because of the growing pressure to find Arthur's killer and restore tranquility to the town again. The economic unrest weighed heavily across the country and the region which added more suspicion and watchful eyes. It could have been anybody who killed Arthur Floyd, but one thing was certain. Whoever they pinned the murder on was going to hang.

Frederick Walton followed the sheriff and the Floyd brothers to Phoebe's cabin. No one uttered a word until a hard rap against the cabin's door alerted Phoebe who had finally drifted off to sleep. She jerked awake and called aloud.

"Who's there?" Her voice was scratchy.

"Phoebe, it's Mr. Walton. Come on out. Sheriff Baker is here and wants to talk to you."

Phoebe hesitated for a moment. Her hands were trembling as she answered in a shaky voice. "Yes, sir. I--I'll be right there."

Phoebe rolled out of bed, her limbs still achy from the fall in the cemetery and the mad dash back to the cabin. She placed one foot in front of the other and slid her feet across the floor toward the door. She reached for the door handle and unlocked the bolt.

All eyes stared at the disheveled black woman standing before them as she opened the door. Her eyelids were swollen, her hair matted and flat against her head. She stood with a slight bend at the waist revealing the back pain and agony that she was experiencing. The Floyd brothers looked at Phoebe with raised brow and tight frowns.

"Phoebe, get some shoes on. You're going to show us where the murder weapon is hidden." William Floyd spoke up before anyone else had a chance to say anything. He was trying to trick Phoebe into telling them something she didn't know. The sheriff already knew what Seymour Prater had told them, but William thought that he could get information out of Phoebe if he showed her where the murder weapon was and scared her into confessing what she knew.

Phoebe didn't know anything, but William Floyd wasn't buying it. Sheriff Baker glared at William and shook his head while Mr. Walton stared in disbelief.

Phoebe became distraught. "But I don't know where no murder weapon is. You got to believe me." She pleaded, her eyes filled with tears.

Sheriff Baker spoke up. "Phoebe, we just want you to tell us what you were doing in the cemetery last night. At Arthur Floyd's grave. We know it was you."

Phoebe shook, her body becoming visibly disturbed at the sheriff's inquiry. "You wouldn't understand, Sheriff."

The sheriff warned her. "Now Phoebe, you could get yourself in a lot of trouble---

Phoebe interrupted, violently shaking her head back and forth. "No, no, no. It's not what you---- Mr. Floyd's ghost. It's after me. It's after me, and you have to believe me. I went to the grave last night to chase those spirits away, and something happened. Something bad happened." Phoebe shouted and screamed, determined to make them believe her.

Mr. Walton placed his hand on Phoebe's arm and motioned for her to sit down. The sheriff and the Floyd brothers closed the cabin door behind them to stop the cold draft from entering the two room shack. Phoebe sat on the edge of the bed and held her face in her hands as she sobbed.

"Phoebe, you've got to stop this nonsense. You can't keep spreading those rumors around the town. The whole black community is scared to death because of what you've been telling them." Sheriff Baker was firm, his voice unwavering.

"I'm not telling them nothing that's not true. Mr. Floyd's spirit is mad. It's mad, I tell you. And it's coming to me. It came to me last night and the night before. I don't know nothing. I just saw him on that floor, but you've got to let me get rid of those evil spirits." Phoebe cried.

"Evil spirits?" William Floyd asked.

"Yes, sir. Evil spirits. Mr. Floyd can't rest because of what was done to him, and now he is mad. He is coming back to get revenge." Phoebe sobbed, her lips quivered.

The sheriff took a deep breath and turned toward the door. "Gentlemen, let's go. Phoebe, if you hear anything, I expect you to let Mr. Walton know. Do you understand?"

"Yes, sir. I do, sir." Phoebe took a deep breath and nodded.

The men exited the shack leaving Phoebe in a state of fright and despair as she wiped tears and sleep from her eyes. The sheriff pushed the door shut and motioned for the others to move away from the cabin where they could not be heard. He then turned and looked directly at Frederick Walton.

"Mr. Walton, keep your eyes on her and make sure she doesn't leave the area for any reason." The sheriff's tone was firm.

"Will do, Sheriff." Mr. Walton agreed.

"William, let's get over to Arthur's place and see if we can find where your friend, Mr. Prater said the murder weapon was." The sheriff ordered.

"But don't you want Phoebe to go?" Mr. Walton asked.

The sheriff shook his head. "I changed my mind. If she knows anything about the case, I don't want her knowing what we find or where I put it until this is over."

The sheriff turned and headed straight for the dead man's store.

Sheriff Baker arrived at the Floyd Place followed by Deputy Phillips. He parked his car at the back of the building and quickly got out of the car, not wasting anymore time as he searched the grounds. If there was a cistern on the outside of the Floyd property, he had never seen it. But the round, man-made water reservoir used to catch and store rainwater was located on the inside, in the basement of the store. Although the sheriff and deputy had already searched the upper floor of the building, they had not searched the basement and the five foot deep receptacle at the bottom of the stairs. If Prater was right, the killers left the murder weapon there.

The sheriff and deputy followed William and Bobby up the steps and pushed the back door open. They hurriedly walked in and passed through Arthur's office before they reached the door leading to the basement. William led the way, flicking on a light switch as he made his way down the stairs, his heavy boots sounding off a hard thump with each step. The cold basement air brushed hard against their faces as they neared the basement floor. They stepped off the last stair step and stood around the empty cistern. Its opening was covered by a wood plank.

Bobby reached for the board and pushed it aside as the men peered over the cistern's edge and into an empty dark tunnel. The sheriff reached into his pocket and pulled out a small flashlight. He flicked it on and pointed the light into the cistern revealing a mostly dry basin except for a small puddle of water near the bottom.

"I don't see anything." Bobby's tone echoed his disappointment, and he leaned back away from the opening.

"Wait, there! There it is! I see it. The water was covering the edge of the handle." William shouted and pointed down into the barrel.

Bobby leaped forward and leaned back across the opening where he now saw what his brother had discovered. The sheriff moved swiftly to the edge and peered over the side. "Yep, there it is."

"It's right where Seymour Prater said it would be and look! I think that's the keys to the front door!" William exclaimed.

The sheriff began to shine the light around the room. "We need something to get down there. We need a shovel or rake. Something to use to fish it out of there."

"Here. There's a hoe and a shovel against that wall." Bobby picked it up and handed it back to Deputy Phillips who was waiting to dig it out while the sheriff held the flashlight.

Deputy Phillips was able to catch the end of the ax against the blade on the hoe and maneuver it out of the water as he slowly lifted it high enough for the sheriff to grab on to. The head of the ax was still partially splattered with the blood and brain matter of Arthur Floyd. The deputy gagged upon seeing the bloody ax and quickly buried his face in his shirt sleeve before he resumed fishing for the store keys.

The sheriff laid the ax down on the basement floor and waited for Deputy Phillips to snag the keys. The deputy fished around the basin and finally managed to capture the large round ring of keys after dropping them three times. Then just as the sheriff grabbed the keys securing them in his hand, a door violently slammed shut somewhere in the store.

All of four of the men jumped. Sheriff Baker whispered. "What the hell was that?"

"I don't know. Sounds like a door. Somebody must be upstairs." William spoke in a low tone.

The sheriff turned off the flashlight, and whispered. "Shhh. We'll hear footsteps if someone's there."

The Floyd brothers remained dead calm, too scared to move or utter a sound. What if the killer had returned to the scene of the crime? After a few minutes of stillness and no noted movement upstairs, the sheriff decided to ease up the side of the basement wall and climb the staircase back to Arthur's office. The deputy was close behind him while William and Bobby stayed at a close distance.

The sheriff inched up the stairs, his Smith & Wesson .357 Magnum unholstered and ready to fire if needed. His feet gently landed on each step, careful not to make a sound. He finally made it to the door opening where he was able to peer out into the room. Nothing appeared to have changed since he and the others had entered the store. In fact, the back door was still slightly ajar, just as Bobby had left it when he was the last one to enter the building.

Sheriff Baker turned to the deputy and motioned for him to follow. He turned the corner leading out of Arthur's office and glanced all around the building. Nothing. The front door still appeared to be locked and secure as it had been days ago. The door slam that they all heard was now a mystery.

The sheriff called out. "Hey, William. Everything looks ok up here."

William exited the basement stairs carrying the ax in his hand with the store keys hanging outside his front pocket. The sheriff pointed at the ax.

"Now that we've got the keys to the store back, let's lock that thing in the safe here. And don't tell anybody that we found it. I know I heard a damn door slam while we were in that basement. The killer may come back for it if he thinks we are in here looking for it. We need somebody to stay here overnight for a few nights. Just to see if anything happens. Me or the deputy will be next door watching the place as well, but two sets of eyes are better than one."

William nodded once. "I'll stay tonight."

See No Evil

Bobby placed the ax into the safe and pushed the door shut, locking it. The men then turned to exit through the back door where they had entered, but just as the deputy reached for the door, the sound of heavy footsteps came barging down the middle aisle toward them. Bobby Floyd froze, unable to move as he listened to the invisible footsteps approaching him from behind. The loud, hurried steps stopped near the entrance to Arthur's office. Bobby looked around at the others.

"Did you hear that?" Bobby asked. His eyes were wide and his face pale.

"Hear what?" William asked.

"Foot---Footsteps. Damn footsteps, that's what." Bobby stuttered. His limbs were rigid, his fists clenched by his side and his body shaking. The leg of his pants was fiercely moving about as he struggled to calm himself.

"No, I didn't hear no footsteps. Brother, I believe your mind is just playing tricks on you. Come on." William laughed it off. The men opened the door and walked out onto the back porch. But just as William started to close the door behind him, an unexpected gust of wind rushed past him with a violent force that slammed the door shut against him. It would be after sunset when William Floyd returned to the store, and the angry spirit that had captured the soul of his murdered brother would be there waiting for him. Watching and waiting through hollow eyes.

Chapter 11

It was well past sunset when William Floyd entered his deceased brother's store. The night sky appeared as a dark, clear canvas with a round full moon suspended in its center. Hours had passed with no further clues as rumors of Arthur Floyd's haunting cast a shadow over the town. Carrollton was fast becoming known as a nesting place for the restless spirits of the dead.

Meanwhile, Frederick Walton attempted to calm members of the black community who had gathered outside his property. Confused and fearing repercussions from their white bosses, many black people had begun to question Phoebe's involvement in the Floyd killing. Whispers echoed throughout the small village located just down the hill from the town square. If Phoebe was being haunted by the dead man's ghost, she might be his killer or know who his killer was. Everyone was demanding answers and now almost half of the community's black residents threatened to abandon their loyalty to Phoebe. With only a handful of family and friends, Phoebe's demise was becoming a reality she wasn't prepared to face. She had been in the wrong place at the wrong time. Guilty only by her presence on the morning that Arthur Floyd lay dead before her eyes, and there was now nothing that she could do about it except beg the help of her elders and cast his tormented soul back into the spirit world.

Frederick Walton stood before a group of fifty people staring hard at him through curious eyes, his feet firmly planted on the edge of the porch steps leading into the grandiose house where Phoebe worked each day caring for the Walton family. He lifted his hands in the air and signaled for the people to listen to him, but it was to no avail as two people in the group began to speak loud, demanding that Mr. Walton hear their pleas.

"You must release this vile person you have living on your property! You will have a curse on your land if you don't listen! The spirits are after her!" A tall, black man with striking, blue eyes stepped forward shaking his fist in the air as he spoke. Mr. Walton froze, unable to move as he listened to the man's declaration. A wave of fear swept over his body sending a ripple of cold chills up his spine until it covered the pores of his scalp. His heart began to beat faster as he forced words from his mouth.

"Listen to me, folks! The sheriff doesn't know who killed Arthur Floyd. Nobody's been charged with a crime here. Not Phoebe, not nobody! Do you hear me? I said, Nobody! Now all you folks go home or go back to minding your own business. And don't come back on this property lest you get shot for trespassing!" Frederick Walton locked eyes with the leader of the group in spite of his fear.

He raised his arms high once more, waving them in the air as he shouted. "Go on, now! Get out of here!"

The black man with the intense, blue eyes hesitated to move. Finally, the crowd slowly began to back away, still keeping their eyes fixed on Walton while some of the others studied the cabin where Phoebe remained hidden. She was locked inside under a mound of blankets, trembling and sweating from the same fever that had ravaged her body within minutes after her escape from the cemetery the night before. Phoebe was under spiritual attack, and she knew it. Without help, she would surely die. She was certain that the spirit of Arthur Floyd was responsible for this, but he was attacking the wrong person.

Phoebe's two sisters quietly sneaked past the crowd and waited near the cabin until all of the others had moved out of sight. Walton saw the women from the front porch steps where he stood. He walked over to the cabin and assisted the two women who had come to see about Phoebe by opening the door while they carried a small kettle of homemade remedies. The herbal aroma filled the small room upon entering. Phoebe rolled over to one side and opened one eye as she pulled the covers down and peeked over her knuckles.

"Phoebe, you got to get up and drink this." Milly, her oldest sister ordered. She pushed the concoction closer to Phoebe who now attempted to sit up on the side of the bed.

"Mr. Walton says you got to get well and come back to work lest he find someone else to take your place. You don't want that."

Phoebe shook her head and put her hands out in front of her, motioning for Milly to give her the herbal remedy that she had carefully brewed. Phoebe held the bowl in her hands and drank slowly. The salty taste caused her to back away and cough, her mouth screwed up in an expression of distaste, but Milly pushed the bowl back toward her mouth. Phoebe hurriedly gulped the drink and managed to get it down while fighting the urge to vomit. Her throat was dry and itchy, but the hot, steamy drink seemed to soothe her sinuses and clear her head momentarily. It was a welcome improvement.

Phoebe looked up at Milly and whispered "thank you". Her eyes spoke louder than her voice could carry at the moment, and the message they carried was one of despair.

"You have to help me, Milly. The spirits are after me." Phoebe cried, wringing her hands over and over while resting them in her lap.

"Yes, I know. The others believe that you are lying. Are you lying, sis?" Milly studied Phoebe.

"How could you doubt me? You know I am not lying? Why would you ask me such things?" Phoebe became agitated, but was too weak to argue.

Milly shook her head. "The others are saying bad things, Phoebe. But I want to believe you. You're my sister."

"Somebody killed Mr. Floyd, but I don't know who." Phoebe leaned forward toward Milly, invading her space. Her lips were pursed together as she spoke.

Milly nodded. "We'll come back to pray over you. We'll send the spirit of Arthur Floyd away. Tonight."

Phoebe nodded and leaned back against the bed. Her eyelids began to feel heavy and slowly fall shut. Then just as they closed, the ghostly face of Arthur Floyd flashed before her. Like a cinematic reel, Arthur's bloody image left its imprint imbedded in her mind. Phoebe prayed. Her lips trembled as she whispered over and over. *Release.* She prayed for release.

William Floyd emptied his pockets on the desk in Arthur's office as he prepared to settle in for the night. He pulled his trousers off and laid them on the chair next to the cot where he would be sleeping. He wouldn't be resting upstairs in Arthur's old bedroom. No, he and Bobby would be taking turns sleeping downstairs for the next several days, maybe even weeks, as they sought to find their brother's killer. And it was time to re-open the store. Life had to return to some type of normalcy if the family business was going to survive. The community had depended on Arthur's store for years. It had provided staple foods and horse tact, farming supplies, and gardening tools that weren't available elsewhere in the small town. Yes, the town depended on Arthur Floyd's store as much as he had depended on them.

William turned back to the cot, positioning himself to sit down. As he leaned backward, his body almost touching the bed, he froze. His body became stiff as he heard the sound of heavy footsteps trampling down the middle aisle of the store. The faint sound of a man's agonizing moans accompanied each step. His heart began to beat fast, and he found it almost impossible to breathe. *Someone was in the store with him. But how?*

William stood up again, careful not to make a sound and reached for his trousers. He quickly slipped them back on and glanced around the dimly lit room, watching and waiting as the footsteps inched closer. Beads of sweat began to break out across William's forehead as he breathed slow, shallow breaths. He felt paralyzed but knew that he had to act quickly. He reached for a flashlight and the .38 revolver on the floor beside him and held it tightly in his hand, his finger resting on the trigger. *Had Arthur's killer returned to kill him too?* William placed his thumb on the gun's hammer. He used extreme caution to remain quiet as he slowly pulled it backward, cocking it into place.

William inched his way toward the door, placing one foot in front of the other. He had left the door slightly open when he had entered the room moments before and now found himself hiding behind it. He glanced through the crack and peered into the open hallway leading to the back of the store's entrance. The room was almost too dark to make out any movement. His eyes settled on the candle that he had left burning in a mason jar on a table near the edge of the hallway. The flickering flame helped to illuminate a path to the front of the store.

The footsteps had ceased to move, and the room was dead silent as William bravely stepped from behind the door. "Who's there? I've got a gun!" William shouted without hesitating. His finger was tightly wrapped around the trigger pull now.

Silence. There was nothing but utter silence. And the room was full of a stillness that seemed to hang from the rafters in a looming prophecy. Something sinister was waiting for William Floyd. It was the evil that had killed his brother. Not in physical form, but in the ghostly shadows of what was once his beloved brother, now hell bent on revenge.

See No Evil

William turned the corner and looked down the aisles where nothing but darkness hung in midair. The shelves were still lined and untouched just as Arthur Floyd had prepared it days before he was murdered.

"Who's there? Show yourself!" William shouted as he moved closer to the front of the store. The beam of the flashlight bounced back and forth off the walls as he aimed and pointed it from side to side.

He stopped in the middle aisle and jerked around shining the flashlight toward the back entrance. His breath was heavy, and his heart raced. He could almost feel it throbbing through his skin as fear crept up his spine and settled on the back of his neck. Every hair on his head seemed to tingle at once as he stood paralyzed just under the hanging light that dangled over the former site of Arthur Floyd's dead body.

"What do you want? Who are you?!" William shouted again, but this time his voice became shrill. His skin crawled with an awareness that he had never felt before. At that moment and with absolute surmise, William Floyd realized that there was no one physically in the store with him. It was something else, and it was watching him. William tried to step backwards, but his feet were numb.

Thump. Thump. Thump.

Footsteps were approaching. Heavy, loud boots that stomped against the floor were pounding their way straight toward him. William desperately tried to move. He struggled to lift his foot, but fear had paralyzed his every movement. He was locked in place as the unseen predator continued to parade up and down the floor, relishing in the terror that it was causing. Slow, then fast.

Thump. Thump, thump. Thump.

William began to scream, shouting with a violent urgency. "Leave me alone! Leave me alone, I say!"

The sound of boots began to shuffle across the wood floor until it came to a halt behind him. It stood suspended in place, and the terror it delivered now controlled William. He began to feel an icy, cold sensation sliding down the center of his head until it ached. His head throbbed with pain as the dangling light bulb above him began to swing back and forth.

A disembodied groan hovered near his ear, and William felt that his heart might explode at any minute if he didn't escape. He dropped the pistol and flashlight at his side and fell to the floor. He gripped the wood floor with his fingertips as he pulled himself away from the murder site, but the disembodied voice continued to get louder. Its words were now clear. *You know.*

William's entire body shook as he struggled to reach the back door. He had to get the hell out of there. A sudden image of Phoebe's face zipped through his mind. She had been telling the truth. The whole time.

As the malevolent messenger hovered above William Floyd, he summoned all his strength and leaped to his feet. His knees ached as he stood up straight and made a sudden dash forward, grabbing the doorknob and twisting it fast and hard. He flung it open and stumbled out onto the back porch. He raced down the steps and ran steadfast toward the sheriff's office.

William pounded on the sheriff's door. "Sheriff! Sheriff, are you there?" The light was on in the small office, but William could not see the sheriff through the front window. He banged on the door again, rattling the glass pane in the window casing. "Sheriff!"

Sheriff Baker jerked awake and bolted out of the chair where he had been resting. He swung the door open, slamming it against the wall. "William!"

"Sheriff, I didn't know what else to do. I didn't know where else to go." William kept shaking his head.

"What are you talking about? What's happened?" The sheriff stared back at William, but the fear in William's eyes dominated his ability to focus. He fought back tears.

"Phoebe wasn't lying, Sheriff." William's complexion was ashen.

"What are you saying? That Negro woman has gone mad, William." The sheriff's tone was definitive.

"No. She was telling the truth. I swear it. Something just attacked me back at the store. It had me pinned to the floor, and I couldn't move my feet. I ain't never going back!" William was shaking now, his eyes wild.

The sheriff looked stunned. He spoke barely above a whisper. "What are you saying?"

William looked down at the ground, shaking his head again. He then looked back at the sheriff and locked eyes with him. "I'm saying that place is haunted by *somebody* or *something*, but I ain't never going back in that damn place again."

The sheriff let out a sigh. He stepped aside and motioned for William to sit down in an empty chair. "You know that woman claims to be haunted by the spirit of your dead brother. You know this."

William nodded and looked at the sheriff with a sideways glance. "That's why she was in the graveyard the other night. She was working her voodoo magic to cast the spirit away." William huffed. The sheriff looked confused.

"We're nowhere closer to solving this case than we were before we found the murder weapon." The sheriff scratched the side of his cheek.

"Yeah, but we would have never found the murder weapon if it hadn't been for that Pontotoc man." William responded.

"You mean that prophet man. What's his name?" The sheriff inquired.

"Name is Prater. Seymour Prater." William answered.

The sheriff paused. He began to pace the floor in front of the desk, his right hand resting on the pistol handle sticking out of its holster.

He rubbed his forehead with his left hand as he thought about Seymour Prater and his uncanny ability. Then without warning, a gush of wind blew past him and caught the door that was still resting against the wall. The door swung forward, then slowly back. And again with an inexplicable force, the door slammed past the sheriff brushing the side of his foot. He jumped back and grimaced as he felt the door scrape against the side of his boot.

William jerked backward in the chair, throwing his arms up to cover his face and slammed his head against the wall. In an instant, he regained his composure and looked at the sheriff, waiting to get a confirmation of what he believed was the ghost of Arthur Floyd disturbing the peace.

The sheriff coughed and wiped his face. His eyes were wide with shock and disbelief as he took a moment to catch his breath. There was no wind and no expected stormy weather that would have predicted the sudden gust that they experienced. As ridiculous as it might sound to normal, God-fearing folks, the sheriff now had reason to believe Phoebe Jones and William Floyd's stories. But he sure as hell wasn't one to take on a haunting.

A few seconds later, the sheriff caught his breath. He looked William Floyd square in the face and pointed his finger while he spoke.

"We need to get that Prater man back on the case." The sheriff coughed again as a chill crept over his arms.

William nodded.

"Tomorrow morning-- As soon as the sun comes up, you and Bobby find that man. And find out who the hell killed Arthur Floyd."

Chapter 12

As the sun peeked over the horizon, William and Bobby once again started their journey to visit the mystic in Pontotoc County. A restless night and a dying need to end the turmoil circulating around Carrollton fueled the two men's quest to find answers.

Finally after more than three hours of traveling, the men reached Pontotoc and William remembered the directions to Seymour Prater's home. He followed Highway 342 until he reached the familiar dirt path known as Cooper's Crossing Road where he turned and followed it toward the Prater Farm.

The men drove over the last hill toward the house. In the distance they could see a man getting into a car near the same front porch where they had sat the week before. Seymour Prater had already started his day with visitors from one hundred miles away seeking help from the man known for his "radio mind".

As William and Bobby parked the car, the unknown man raised his hand and waved hello as he put the car in reverse. Seymour Prater recognized the Floyd's car and remembered their visit just a few days before. He placed the milk pail that he held in one hand back down on the porch floor and walked to the edge where he greeted the men as they exited the car.

"Hello, Gentlemen. What brings you back to Pontotoc?" Prater's tone was warm, but inquisitive. He motioned for them to join him on the porch.

"Good morning, Mr. Prater." William answered and started up the steps as Bobby followed behind him. He took a seat directly across from Prater while Bobby leaned against a porch column.

"Mr. Prater, the sheriff of Carrollton sent us back to see you." He paused for a moment and looked at Seymour Prater who offered no comment but studied William's face without blinking an eye. A flood of insight was pouring into Prater's mind, images that he didn't want to see and yet he couldn't stop them.

"We've got real trouble in our town, Sir. Bad trouble. And we don't know how to tell you this cause you're gonna think we are crazy, but it's true." Bobby interjected.

Seymour Prater felt a cold chill creeping over his body. His head began to tingle as the images played over and over in his mind like a silent movie. "What do you need from me?" Prater knew before he asked, but waited for their disclosure.

Bobby leaned away from the porch column and put his hands in his pants pocket. He looked Prater in the eye. "After we left here last week, we went back to my brother's store, and we found the murder weapon exactly where you told us it would be."

Prater nodded and answered in a matter-of-fact tone. "Yes." His calmness indicated his lack of wonderment. Years of being right had diminished the element of surprise when people confessed that his predictions had been true.

Prater was a humble man, but he was a believer in God, and it was no surprise to him who was responsible for his supernatural talents.

"But something else is happening to us. It's something that we don't understand." William spoke up now; his need to find answers was evident. He held his hands tight, resting them in his lap while rubbing his thumbs hard against each other. Prater noticed the body language.

"The Negro woman knows the killers." Prater spoke quick and precise.

Bobby Floyd's body jerked to attention. "She knows who killed our brother?"

Prater shook his head. "I see your brother's killers. They ran out the back door on the night of the murder. Your brother's death was over money. Somebody owed him money."

William shifted in his chair. "I don't understand. How does Phoebe Jones know his killer?"

Prater's eyes were now closed as he rubbed the side of his head, massaging his temples in a circular fashion. "She is sick. The woman is sick with a fever. She knows the killers, but she doesn't know that they committed the crime."

"Tell us their names. Please. We need a name." Bobby begged.

Prater hesitated. "I cannot."

"What do you mean, you 'cannot'?" William raised his voice, his anger and frustration now evident and taking control.

Prater became agitated. Something didn't feel right. The same familiar feeling that he had days before was now resurfacing, and this time it was stronger than before. Nausea consumed him. His stomach churned and filled with knots that ached like tiny bee stings covering his abdomen. He rested his hand against his midriff and pressed down with his palm as his mouth began to water with the urge to vomit.

"I cannot-- Seymour paused and looked up at William who was now out of his chair and standing right before him.

"What good is your gift if you can't tell us who you see? You see two people. You told us where the murder weapon was, and you even know about Phoebe, but you can't tell us a name? People are going mad in our town, Mr. Prater. You are our only hope!" William shouted, his voice echoing in the distance.

Prater's wife, Rachel overheard the loud scene from inside the house and walked to the screen door. She pushed the door open and peered out, her eyebrows in a furrow and her mouth in a frown of disapproval as she glared at the Floyd brothers. The short, small framed woman held onto the screen doorframe. The men remained quiet, not daring to utter a word. She refused to move from her position as she displayed the protective nature that she often assumed around people who questioned her husband's abilities. It was only after her husband broke the silence that she backed away and closed the screen door.

"I've told you all that I can. My gift is from the Lord, Gentlemen. But I cannot always control what I see. And even if I could tell you the name of your brother's killer, do you think that sheriff would hang somebody without any more evidence than that?" Prater sighed and wiped his mouth on the sleeve of his shirt.

William and Bobby kept their gaze fixed on the prophet whom they had put their faith in, hoping for answers that would solve a murder mystery and put an end to the horrific haunting that overshadowed the town. William Floyd and Phoebe Jones had no peace because of their exposure to Arthur Floyd's restless spirit, but the spirit that they both experienced wasn't the man that had once lived and worked in the small town of Carrollton, Mississippi. No, the spirit represented something else. It represented darkness and the transformation that consumed his spirit when the living stole his life. It represented the revenge of the wicked souls who still lived free, uncharged and unpunished for their crimes.

William began to back away. He turned to face Bobby and pointed with his index finger toward the car. "We better go."

"What? We just drove three hours for this? No." Bobby didn't move.

Prater remained quiet and observed the two men. He saw despair in their eyes, and although he felt compassion for their situation, he knew the consequences of his gift and the dangers that it could bring forth. Without physical evidence to back his supernatural insights, his mystic powers were useless. And he could not give the men what they wanted from him. They wanted Seymour Prater to be the judge and the jury for the guilty party who murdered their brother. It was a role he wasn't prepared to fill, but in the eyes of the Floyd brothers and many others who came seeking Seymour Prater's miraculous messages, he was a direct link to a power straight from God.

"Gentlemen, wait." Prater stood up and followed behind William. He stopped at the corner of the porch and stood beside Bobby Floyd who had not moved in spite of William's affirmation that it was time to leave. He placed one hand against the porch post and gazed out across the open farm fields that included hundreds of green, lush acreage and a natural flowing creek. It was nature's beauty and a necessary focus at times when Prater needed the tranquil scenery for meditation.

"There's one other thing that I can tell you about the night your brother died." Prater broke his gaze across the fields and turned to lock eyes with William Floyd. William froze where he stood, his full attention on Prater.

"You know the path behind your brother's store?" Prater asked. He slid his hands down the suspenders fastened to his trousers and rested his hands in his pants pocket.

Bobby leaned forward and looked around his brother's left side which was blocking his view of Prater. He quickly answered for them both. "Yeah, we know about it."

Prater nodded and chewed his lower lip. "Follow that path, Gentlemen, and you'll find your killers."

"But, but that path---it leads to the cemetery and the Walton Farm. We've already been there!" William exclaimed.

A breeze blew past Prater blowing his wavy, brown locks of hair forward. Prater removed his hands from his pockets and reached for the hat hanging on the back of the chair. He placed it on his head and turned to the men.

"Follow the footsteps of Phoebe Jones. Good day, Gentlemen." Seymour Prater tipped his hat, then turned and disappeared behind the screen door.

Chapter 13

The crickets seemed to chirp louder and nightfall moved fast, casting a shadow upon the small town earlier than usual after William and Bobby arrived back in Carrollton. The brothers said little to each other during the drive, but both of them agreed that the sheriff needed to accompany them along the path behind Arthur's store. If the path was going to lead to Arthur's killers as Seymour Prater predicted, then the

See No Evil

sheriff and the deputy had to know about it, and they damn sure had to be there.

The day had turned to twilight as William and Bobby drove around the courthouse square and parked the car in front of Sheriff Baker's office. The men got out of the car and walked to the door. William noticed the sheriff sitting at the desk in his usual style, feet propped on the corner of a wood chair in front of him while he read The Conservative, the town's newspaper service located just a few minutes away in Winona, Mississippi.

Sheriff Baker quickly slid his feet off of the chair and leaned forward to stand when he heard the engine turn off outside the office door. He glanced up and looked out the front window. Immediately upon seeing William and Bobby, he made his way around the desk and walked to the door where he met the Floyd brothers before they could even turn the doorknob to go inside. He pulled the door open and greeted them with a look of anticipation, his eyes fixed in an inquisitive stare.

"You made it back." The sheriff stated the obvious and waited for a response.

William rubbed his fingers across his forehead. "The Prater man told me to follow the path behind the store. He says it will lead us to our killers."

The sheriff paused. He thought about this latest clue and mentally addressed the possibility of solving the case based on Prater's tip.

"That path leads to several different areas. It leads to the Walton Farm where that Negro woman lives. It leads to the cemetery by the church where Arthur is buried, and it leads to the Negro community. What the hell are we supposed to be looking for?"

William shook his head.

"That doesn't help us much, but it's another clue that we have to follow. And we'll have to do this without Deputy Phillips. He's been over at the funeral home all day with the McCain family. Bobby, grab one of those flashlights over there."

Bobby picked up an extra flashlight for William and headed out the door as the sheriff locked up and followed behind him. About fifty yards from the sheriff's office, he turned and started for the path that was predicted to lead to justice for Arthur Floyd. A man's unjustified death at the hands of a murderer was about to be avenged because of The Mississippi Mystic, Seymour Prater and his undeniable supernatural gifts.

Prater had "seen" the killer's jacket splattered with blood and lying in the brush over the fence that separated the dirt path from the Walton property. But he had hesitated to disclose the information. Prater knew that someone would surely hang for Arthur Floyd's death, and if he couldn't prove beyond any reasonable doubt that his supernatural ability was in fact a fool proof means of identifying a man's killer, then he no longer wanted a man's guilt or innocence weighting heavily on his conscience. He was damned either way. He believed that it was his obligation to reveal any helpful information that he could. Furthermore, he believed that it was a destined responsibility that he had come to accept as a young boy, and now there were severe consequences if his predictions were wrong. The Floyd case was different than anything he had witnessed before, and because of that Seymour Prater felt more compelled than ever to use his supernatural talents as God had directed him to. From three hours away, Prater "tuned" in to the town of Carrollton, Mississippi and the Floyd brothers as they searched along the dirt path with the sheriff at their side.

William and the sheriff followed Bobby a short distance away. Chills crept up William's arms as he stopped near the back porch steps. The sheriff walked up behind him.

"What's going on? Why'd you stop?" The sheriff asked. He placed his hand on the .38 in the holster fastened to his waist.

William froze, and yelled at Bobby. "Hey, Bobby, wait! Come back here." William's face had turned ghostly white, his eyes now wide.

Bobby turned and rushed back to his brother's side. "What's going on?"

William felt faint but managed to raise his hand and point toward the back window of the store. There in the window was a shadow, watching and observing the men as if it had an expectation. An expectation of something that they would find.

The sheriff suddenly jumped and attempted to hide behind shrubbery, but the shadow continued to watch. "What the hell is that?" Sheriff Baker was immediately overwhelmed with a fear that he wasn't accustomed to fighting. He realized that whatever he was seeing at that moment was not human.

William could not feel his body. He was literally frozen with terror as he recalled the experience that he had with the shadow just a few days before. With a sudden thrust forward, Bobby dashed toward William and grabbed his arm, breaking him away from the fright that had paralyzed him. The men then rushed to join the sheriff behind the shrubbery.

They watched the shadow begin to move across the window pane. It slithered against the glass like a snake searching for a warm body to devour as it faded in and out, unable to find an opening to escape.

Bobby's mouth hung open. His voice cracked as he spoke. "We've got to get on that damn path like Prater told us to. That's what Phoebe has been trying to tell us, ain't it? That's the ghost, and it won't leave until this is over."

William's tone was almost breathless as he mumbled aloud. "Yeah, it tried to kill me."

"On my signal, let's get the hell out of here and head toward the Walton Farm. You ready?" The sheriff ordered.

William nodded once, his eyes moistened with fear while Bobby massaged his legs, trying to stop them from shaking. The sheriff began to count to three.

"One, Two—

Just then, a violent force crashed against the interior door slamming it open against the outside wall. The men fell to the ground and covered their ears as a piercing scream echoed around them. It darted back and forth in front of them, an invisible swishing noise that wasn't about to let up. The sheriff shouted to the Floyd brothers.

"Go now! Run!" The sheriff dashed behind William and followed them onto the dirt path.

The men raced forward with all their might until the store was now a quarter mile in the distance. William stopped to catch his breath. He quickly looked all around him watching and waiting for anything lurking beyond the fence line as dusk was taking over and darkness was making it impossible to see beyond the trees. And the only sound that could be heard was the lyrics of the tree frogs as they chirped in unison.

A sudden burst of cool wind rustled the leaves and startled Sheriff Baker. He fumbled with the flashlight, searching for the switch to turn it on. Finally, his fingers found the button, and he quickly aimed the flashlight's beam to the left and right of them as he pointed it toward the fence. There was nothing there. Nothing that he could see, but he could hear it. He could hear it breathing. William and Bobby flicked their flashlights on as well and shined them up the path ahead of them.

"We're being followed." Sheriff Baker whispered.

"In the name of Christ, you don't mean it." Bobby frantically whispered back.

The men stayed quiet, no one daring to move as they waited to see what or who was following them. Then the entity began to take on a different persona. A persona that matched the spirit of Arthur Floyd and not the evil one they had feared before. At the same time, the men all heard the sound of footsteps shuffling along the dirt path toward them and an agonizing lament until the sound ceased a few yards in front of them.

William Floyd began to sweat, his stomach becoming queasy as he felt the ghostly presence. It was something he could not see, but his body sensed it in the most profound way as if he could now hear words it was trying to convey.

"Follow that sound." William whispered. He raised his hand and motioned with the flashlight toward the ditch a few yards in front of them. Scared beyond anything he had ever imagined, he knew he had to find the courage to confront the spirit that was torturing him and put an end to the haunting. He had to find his brother's killer.

Meanwhile, back in Pontotoc County, Seymour Prater sat in the same wood chair on the front porch where he had counseled hundreds of people over the years and concentrated on the scenes he was receiving from Carrollton, Mississippi. He leaned forward and closed his eyes. He rested his elbows on his knees and began to massage his eyelids with the tips of his fingers. As he focused on the Floyd brothers, he could see what was happening at that very moment. And he knew that the ghost of Arthur Floyd was now leading them straight to the abandoned coat that was saturated with his ultimate sacrifice.

Chapter 14

William Floyd jumped across the three foot wide ditch, stumbling as he landed on the bank across from the road. Bobby and Sheriff Baker stood opposite facing him.

"Shine the light here. I think I saw something over there near the fence." William said as he pointed to the left.

The sheriff and Bobby raised their flashlights toward the left of William. Just as the light's beam made contact with the fence, the men saw the sleeve of the blood splattered beige coat tucked beneath the brush.

"That looks like blood! Pull it out of there, William!" The sheriff shouted. He looked down at the ground and searched for a stick to pick it up with, but William was too fast.

William reached down and carefully picked the coat up with his fingertips. The men grimaced and coughed from the rancid smell that filled the air. Although the bloody stains were dry, the putrefied stench still lingered.

"Here. Put it on the end of this stick." Sheriff Baker bent down and picked up a thin, tree limb and extended it across the ditch. He waited for William to hang the coat on the end.

The sheriff retrieved the coat and wasted no time examining it while Bobby held the flashlight in place illuminating the scene. The sheriff turned the coat around and noticed the two front pockets. He patted the pockets, feeling for contents and then carefully slid a finger inside. As his index finger slid across the inside right pocket, he suddenly felt a crinkled and wadded piece of paper.

"Wait! There's something in here." The sheriff quickly pulled the wadded paper out and checked the other pocket before unrolling the round, crumpled ball.

As he spread the wrinkled paper out before him, his eyes widened with curiosity as he stared down at an invoice from Arthur Floyd's store. The invoice was billed to Charles Wood, a local laborer at the Walton Farm.

Sheriff Baker mumbled aloud to himself. "Charles Wood. Who is Charles Wood?" He ran his finger along his lips as he studied the invoice. A bloody jacket that belonged to Charles

Wood with an invoice showing an unpaid balance to Arthur Floyd.

Sheriff Baker cleared his throat. He turned and started back the way they had come, his destination certain now. "Let's go, Men. I've got to get back to the office and get the car. I think we've got our killer."

William and Bobby quickly followed the sheriff. "Who is it, Sheriff?" Bobby asked.

The sheriff bit his lower lip before he answered. "It's one of the Walton hands. And if I'm right, it's also the same man who wanted to shut Phoebe up one way or another."

William stared at him with raised eyebrows. "But Prater told us that Phoebe didn't know anything."

"Yeah, but he didn't know that. This is finally starting to make sense now, but if your fortune teller friend is right, that would mean that he has a brother who helped him kill Arthur." As the sheriff walked fast toward town, the ghost of Arthur Floyd rushed past them creating a burst of wind that slammed against them with a hard, chilling force.

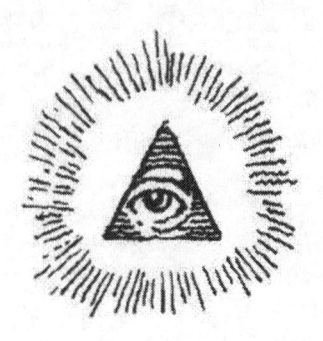

Chapter 15

Bobby stumbled forward almost falling to the ground. He regained his footing and turned to see William's face ghostly white again. The sheriff stopped and turned back to check on the brothers.

"William, come on. It's almost over now." Bobby pleaded as William seemed unable to move forward. The sheriff walked toward him.

"William, it's just the wind, for Christ's sakes. Let's go." The sheriff said with aggravation.

William looked at the sheriff with a sudden rage in his eyes. "You know damn well what it is. And it's coming to get us." William's tone was not his own.

"Bobby, what the hell is going on?" The sheriff became more frustrated as the seconds ticked by, but William seemed to take on the persona of someone else.

"I don't have time for this. Bobby, you deal with your brother. I'm going to the Walton Farm, and I'm making an arrest." Sheriff Baker began to jog down the fourth of a mile trek to Main Street. He still carried the bloody jacket hanging on the end of the tree branch.

When the sheriff reached the end of the path, he sped up and raced as fast as he could run past the Floyd store and toward his office. He ran straight for the front door and unlocked it. He swung the door open fast and jerked the keys to the car off the wall peg before grabbing an extra set of handcuffs out of his desk drawer. He jumped in the car and sped down the street. As he passed the Floyd store, he intentionally avoided looking into the front windows.

Bobby struggled to get William calmed down and aware of his surroundings. The terror was real and it was taking over the body of William Floyd as he fought to maintain his sanity each time he encountered the paranormal. He had never been exposed to the supernatural world, nor had any reason to believe in it. Until now.

The men continued down the trek to the Walton Farm which was only another half mile walk. By the time the sheriff pulled into the main drive leading to the Walton house, William and Bobby were entering the outer gates of the property near the old cemetery where Arthur lay buried.

Sheriff Baker parked the car and walked up the front porch steps to the house. He hammered the door with his fist. "Mr. Walton, Sheriff Baker here!"

Walton was resting in the men's parlor and enjoying a cigar. He quickly rose to his feet and made his way to the front foyer where he opened the door to see Sheriff Baker with a frown and a look of determination in his eyes.

Mr. Walton opened the screen door. "Good evening, Sheriff. How can I help you?"

The sheriff greeted Mr. Walton with a nod. "Good evening. I'm here to make an arrest, Sir."

"An arrest? What the devil for?" Mr. Walton looked stunned.

"One of your laborers is wanted for the murder of Arthur Floyd." The sheriff answered with a firm and unwavering tone.

Mr. Walton's mouth fell open for a brief second, and he began to stutter. "Well, Wh- wh- who in the name of God would do such a thing?"

Several of the Negro laborers now peeked from behind open doors in an effort to hear the conversation from several feet away. They all watched to see what happened next. Although the cabins were too far from the main house for the eavesdroppers to hear any voices, Phoebe

Jones didn't let it deter her as she slipped around the door and snuck her way closer to the Walton's front porch.

"Charles. Charles Wood. And I wanna question his brother again. Robert Wood. I'm here to arrest them both. Where are they?"

Mr. Walton felt the blood drain from his face as he thought about the possibility of Arthur Floyd's killer practically under his nose. Living in his backyard. His heart began to race. "They're in their cabins. In the back. But wait. Let me get my gun." Walton turned and disappeared inside the house for a couple of minutes before he returned with his Winchester Model 21, 12 gauge Double Barrel shotgun loaded and ready to deal with a murderer.

As the sheriff hurriedly walked past Mr. Walton and made his way toward the back of the property, he pulled his sidearm out, cocked the hammer back, and rested his finger on the trigger pull. Frederick Walton followed close behind.

"It's the middle cabin on the opposite end of Phoebe's place." Mr. Walton confirmed his residence at the farm. He then stopped and waited for Charles Wood to come out.

The sheriff rapped on the door. "Charles Wood. Come on out here!" The sheriff shouted then rapped again on the door.

Inside the cabin, Charles Wood knew the end was here for him. There was no more running. No more hiding. And he had been too sloppy. It wasn't a planned killing, but he saw an opportunity, and he took it. He owed Floyd money, but he had no intentions of settling his debt.

Phoebe had seen him wandering down the path late that night. She just happened to be awake when she heard his footsteps walking past

See No Evil

her cabin. She peeked out the front door like she always did, always watching and listening to everything. Minding other people's business even at times when it wasn't safe. She could be a witness, but Phoebe never realized what she had seen. She didn't realize that she had seen Arthur's killer walking past her cabin and on his way to commit murder. And although his brother had helped him dispose of the murder weapon and hide the bloody jacket, it was him that had delivered the fatal blows that split Arthur Floyd's skull nearly in half. He had been the one who had unmercifully stared down at the lifeless, bleeding body of a deaf man known by all of Carrollton as "good ole' Arthur". His brother would be free if he kept his mouth shut and didn't tell the sheriff about his brother's part in the murder, but he knew he was going to die.

Without a doubt, Charles Wood was going to hang.

Phoebe now stood observing the sheriff and Mr. Walton from a distance. She felt the presence of Arthur Floyd once again surrounding her, but this time was different. Her fear was subsiding as she realized the end of the haunting was finally in sight.

William and Bobby Floyd watched from the edge of Phoebe's cabin while Mr. Walton positioned himself on the other side of Charles Wood's shack. The sheriff prepared to shoot the lock off the door, aiming his pistol toward the keyhole when suddenly the door slammed open from the inside.

Charles Wood fell backwards against the floor as an invisible force hurled him toward the wall. Then right before the sheriff's eyes, Arthur Floyd's killer began to rise off the floor, his six foot tall frame limp with his feet dangling in mid-air. He gasped and coughed as the breath was being choked out of him.

The sheriff began to shout. "Charles Wood, you are under arrest for the murder of Arthur Floyd!" Then just as quickly as his feet had lifted into the air, Charles Wood collapsed onto the floor. The atmosphere around them became dead silent, and the stillness was an eerie reminder of the deaf world that Arthur Floyd once knew.

The sheriff moved forward to place the handcuffs around Charles Wood's wrists. He jerked the metal cuffs off the side of his holster and quickly slapped both bands on each wrist, locking the cuffs into place. When the lock clicked shut, Phoebe Jones felt a sudden release as she sensed the spirit of Arthur Floyd rising up and away from her. This was the last moment of her torture, and the last night of her nightmares. She closed her eyes for a moment and breathed deep. Tonight, she would sleep well again.

Seymour Prater opened his eyes and stared out into the darkness that surrounded him now. He had lost track of time and realized that he had been observing the Floyds for the past hour. His hands were cold as he stood up and stretched his legs. He rubbed his eyes one last time and looked out at the stars twinkling in the distance before him. He nodded to himself in agreement for the help that he had provided to the Floyds. Justice could now be served and a restless soul could now find peace.

With a slight grin on his face, The Mississippi Mystic mumbled aloud as he turned to walk inside. "I see, I see."

The End

L. Sydney Fisher

Do YOU Believe?

See No Evil

SEYMOUR PRATER
"The Mississippi Mystic"

The True Accounts

L. Sydney Fisher

Ghastly Slaying Haunts Town

The mysterious death of country merchant, Arthur Floyd was recorded in a Carrollton, Mississippi newspaper in 1931 and stated that the death had never been explained. The writer, Susie James, gave the following account.

"The neighbors felt that the Floyd place was haunted because of the unsolved murder. Mr. Floyd, who was deaf, was killed in his store, a piece of peppermint candy clutched in his hand. Because of the late hour of the crime, folks said that he must have known his killer(s). It was said in the neighborhood that the authorities thought there may have been two attackers. A member of the Floyd family consulted a psychic from Pontotoc on the off chance that he could help solve the case. The psychic told the Floyds that they could find the murder weapon in the cistern in Arthur Floyd's yard. Robert Floyd, a brother of Arthur Floyd stated that the sheriff found it, as well as the keys to the store. The psychic also said that the killers had a dark complexion and were brothers. Some of the people questioned were, in fact, brothers, but they all provided an alibi and were dismissed as a suspect in the case. The murder was never solved."

NOTE: This headline story was the inspiration for this book, *See No Evil.* **Six months of research and preparation was involved in this project.**

This headline story is believed to have been printed in *The Conservative,* **a newspaper based in Winona, Mississippi that served the Carrollton town during this time.**

L. Sydney Fisher

The Lost Colt Revolver

On December 18, 1925 at approximately 11:00 a.m., in Aberdeen, Mississippi, the home of eight year-old Dr. Thomas Paine, Jr. (now living in Nashville, Tennessee) caught fire destroying much of the second floor. With the help of neighbors and friends, most of the first floor contents were salvaged. But Thomas Paine's father owned a World War I Army Colt revolver that had gone missing from a downstairs closet.

About two months later, Mr. Paine, Sr. traveled to Pontotoc with his eight year-old son, Thomas, Jr. to "see about getting his pistol back." They drove up to the farmhouse where Seymour Prater invited them to sit down on the porch. After a few minutes of friendly chatter that included conversation about the weather and crops, Thomas Paine's father stated his business for the visit.

Seymour Prater asked a few questions about the pistol such as a description and where it was kept. He sat quiet for a few minutes and then he began to describe the man who had taken the pistol. He asked Mr. Paine, Sr. if he recognized anyone by that description and the man indicated with a nod and verbal "Yes". After a few more minutes of friendly banter, Mr. Paine, Sr. thanked Seymour Prater and departed.

When Mr. Paine, Sr. returned to Aberdeen, Mississippi, he walked down the street to the guilty man's house and demanded his pistol back. The thief then handed it over.

Although Thomas Paine, Jr. was just a boy when he witnessed Seymour Prater's phenomenal gift, he never forgot it. Years later when asked about his experience, he commented. "I have pondered, puzzled, and wondered all my life about Mr. Prater's God-given gift. He was a remarkable man."

Note: Research uncovered additional information about this story. According to other testimony, Mr. Paine, Sr. approached the wrong neighbor and accused him of stealing the pistol. The neighbor became infuriated and almost started a fight with Mr. Paine who now realized that he was at the wrong location. He then confronted a neighbor whose home was closer to his own and found the stolen pistol, but the falsely accused neighbor never forgave Mr. Paine for the insult.

Source: Tombigbee Country Magazine, September 2009, #116

Who Stole My Mule?

Ms. Nell Loden of Mantachie, Mississippi remembers a time when her grandfather who lived in the Dorsey, Mississippi community lost a gray mule that was one of his most prized possessions. After searching for the mule, her grandfather was unable to find it and became convinced that it had been stolen. He had heard of a man named Seymour Prater from Pontotoc County who could find lost objects and decided to seek his help.

When her grandfather arrived, he said that Prater told him that his mule had "not been stolen". Prater described the place where the mule could be found near a creek and a certain type of bridge. He also described a tree so vividly that her grandfather was able to identify the location without fail. When her grandfather returned home, he immediately went to the spot described by Seymour Prater, and he found the mule exactly where Prater said it would be.

Source: Tombigbee Country Magazine, September 2009, #116

See No Evil

The Runaway Girl

Word of Seymour Prater's talents spread in great distances across the Southeast and as far as New York City when a traveling salesman advised a grief-stricken father to come to Prater for help.

The man traveled hundreds of miles to the Prater Farmhouse and met with Prater. When Prater was told about the girl who had left home days before, he sat down, propped his elbows on his knees, covered his face with his hands, and began to say, "I see, I see." Prater then described the restaurant where the girl was now working with exceptional detail. The father was able to recognize the restaurant because of Prater's descriptions and days later, the man was reunited with his daughter.

L. Sydney Fisher

Diamonds are a Chicken's Worst Friend

Once upon a time, a lady who lived on North Madison Street in Tupelo, Mississippi lost the set from a diamond ring. Unable to locate the missing diamond, she contacted Seymour Prater in nearby Pontotoc County for help.

Prater told her that when she had thrown the dirty water out in the back yard after washing dishes, the set had fallen out, and a hen had swallowed it. The lady then went back home and began to kill her chickens hoping to find the diamond, but not one of the chickens she killed possessed the missing diamond.

She then traveled back to the Prater Farmhouse and consulted with Seymour Prater again who advised her that there was one chicken left roosting on its nest in the henhouse. Sure enough after entering the henhouse, the lady found the guilty chicken, killed it, and found her diamond that had settled in the chicken's gizzard.

Seymour Prater's daughter, Ms. Jessie Prater Montgomery of Starkville, Mississippi commented that "it took two visits to see my father, but she wiped out her whole flock of chickens and found her diamond."

Source: Tombigbee Country Magazine, September 2009, #116

L. Sydney Fisher

A Dead's Man Secret

A man from Shannon, Mississippi, who always kept his money hidden, died without telling anyone where his secret hiding place was located. One of the man's two sons decided to visit Seymour Prater who told them that the money was buried under a plank in the shed that housed the car. Sometime later, the second son visited Seymour Prater, and Prater told him the same story. The second son then returned to the shed and the secret hiding place that belonged to his dead father. He searched the shed and after several minutes, he uncovered the plank described by Seymour Prater to find nothing but an empty hole. The finding and the reality that the first brother had not shared the inheritance caused a rift between the two brothers.

See No Evil

The Missing Wedding Ring

A neighbor who lived next door to Seymour Prater's daughter lost her wedding ring. She kept it in a powder box on her dresser.

One day when Seymour Prater came to visit his daughter, the neighbor came over to see Mr. Prater and ask for his help in finding her ring. He described the person who had stolen the ring but never mentioned the guilty person's name. The neighbor recognized who Mr. Prater described and then wrote a letter to the woman's husband. When the husband opened the letter and read the neighbor's message, he confronted his wife and found out that she had, in deed, stolen the ring. He made his wife mail the ring back to the neighbor that day!

L. Sydney Fisher

A Minister's Mercy

During the Great Depression, a minister known for helping the poor in faraway places, found that a large side of meat was missing from his smokehouse. Suspecting his neighbor, the minister consulted Seymour Prater and learned that his suspicions were correct. But Mr. Prater told him that it was his neighbor's first theft and that he had stolen the meat out of desperation because his children were hungry.

Seymour Prater advised the minister to take the family more food to help them through the hard times they were experiencing. The minister felt much compassion and after leaving the Prater Farm, he went to the poor family's home and gave them more food.

See No Evil

Asleep Under the Tree

Once upon a time, a small child wandered away from home late one afternoon. The family was frantic in their search. They called on the area neighbors and friends for help in the search but were unable to find the missing child. Desperate and weary, they decided to seek the "Pontotoc Seer".

They hurried to the Prater Farm and within minutes, Seymour Prater told them that the child was near the house and asleep by a tree. The family rushed back to their home and followed the directions that Seymour Prater had given them. After a short time, the family was relieved to find the child still sleeping under the tree, right where Seymour Prater had told them.

L. Sydney Fisher

Follow the Tracks

Once upon a time, a man who lived in another part of Pontotoc County miles away from Seymour Prater, lost a Jersey cow from his property. In spite of the man's attempts to locate the lost cow, he wasn't able to find it until he came to Mr. Prater for help.

Seymour Prater was able to describe a beautiful tree on the back side of his pasture and told him that the fence wire was cut near it. The man was confused since he did not remember such a tree, but he thanked Mr. Prater and vowed to search for the tree and the cut wire. He then returned to his property and began his search near the area that Seymour had described. To his surprise, he found the cut fence wire near the tree that Prater had described along with the hoof

See No Evil

prints that led him straight to the discovery of the lost Jersey cow.

L. Sydney Fisher

The Stolen Coat

Once upon a time, a young man's home was robbed just days after he graduated from Pontotoc High School in the same town where Seymour Prater lived. His graduation suit and all of his other clothes were stolen. The young man knew of Mr. Prater's supernatural powers and decided to visit him to see if he could help solve the mystery of the stolen clothes.

The man explained his situation to Mr. Prater who then threw his head back, closed his eyes, and remained silent for a few minutes before he disclosed the description of the two people who had stolen the young man's clothes. Mr. Prater offered no encouragement for recovering the lost clothes, but he did say that the young man would recover a couple of the stolen items at a later time.

Mr. Prater's prediction turned out to be correct because over a year later, a friend of the young man advised him that he had seen his coat at a house approximately two miles from his home. The sheriff was then notified, and he recovered the coat and arrested the person who had stolen it. The young man never forgot Seymour Prater's extraordinary powers and often commented that Mr. Prater's abilities "bordered on the supernatural".

"I see, I see."

Seymour Prater's reputation and fame spread across the South as hundred and even thousands of people paid homage to the "Pontotoc Seer". Some traveled to visit him, following their curious urges to test the prophet's powers.

One such story came from a lady who wanted to test Prater's abilities. She didn't have any lost articles to locate, so she asked him to describe where she lived. Seymour Prater then advised her to remain quiet as his eyes seemed to become fixed on a scene faraway and invisible to everyone except him. In a few moments, he responded in a low, but confident tone.

"I see a two-story house facing east, with white columns and a big porch going around the front and the side of the house. It is in the south part of town."

Mr. Prater was correct. There were no dramatic descriptions, but he spoke with authority. He told her that he had "always had this gift, and he had no doubts at all that it was especially given to him by God, in order to help others."

L. Sydney Fisher

Another Lost Mule

Once upon a time, Seymour Prater's brother, Jeff had a young mule that strayed from his farm in the Pleasant Grove Community of Pontotoc, Mississippi. After riding by horseback for several days in search of his mule and getting no information from anyone in the neighborhood, Jeff decided to consult Seymour for help.

Seymour advised Jeff to go west because he said that he could see someone plowing the mule along the roadside at that very moment! Seymour told his brother that he could not determine if the person with the mule was black or white, but he was certain that the mule was there because he could see him.

Jeff saddled two horses and asked Seymour to go with him. After traveling some distance, Jeff recognized his mule being plowed along the roadside by a Negro woman. He claimed his mule, took him from the plow, and led him home.

L. Sydney Fisher

Supernatural Eavesdropping

Once upon a time, a man who lived in Monroe County, Mississippi sought the help of Seymour Prater for a personal matter. He traveled to Tupelo, Mississippi to see Mr. Prater in his office. His son also accompanied him on the trip, but asked his father if he really thought that the "old man could tell him anything". He continued to make remarks during the ride that were not complimentary about the "fortune teller".

Later when they arrived at Mr. Prater's office, Mr. Prater looked at this young man, whom he had never seen before, and said--

"You are a nice-looking young man, but you don't have a good opinion of me. You made some ugly remarks about me to your father on your way up here. You should not have done that. You didn't know me. So be more careful about your remarks next time."

The young man was immediately overwhelmed with embarrassment and convinced that Seymour Prater "really could tell things".

L. Sydney Fisher

The Mule's White Spot

Once upon a time, a man who lived in West Point, Mississippi posted a notice in the newspaper seeking any known family or friends of Seymour Prater to come forward and contact him. Herman Prater, Seymour's brother saw the newspaper posting and then traveled to the man's house along with his son-in-law, David Warren. After introducing himself to the West Point man, the man began to recount his story of Seymour Prater.

After turning out his stock one Fall day a few years prior, the man lost one of his mules and was unable to locate it later in the Spring. The mule had been missing for several months when one of the man's neighbors told him about Seymour Prater's miraculous powers. The man scoffed at the notion and told his neighbor that he "did not believe in that". Weeks later, his neighbor finally convinced him to seek Seymour's help.

After arriving at the Prater Farm, Mr. Prater offered his help and closed his eyes while he rubbed his forehead. Mr. Prater then told him—

"Yes, I see that the mule is in a sorghum patch about two miles from your house."

The man then told Prater that he knew where the sorghum patch was. Prater then advised him that he might not recognize the mule because its mane had grown out. He told him that he could tell it was his mule because of a white spot at the top of its withers where the collar had worn. The man then replied that the mule did not have a white spot there, but Mr.

Prater was adamant in his final response when he stated to the man—

"You have never noticed it because you kept him sheared at the mane, but now his mane has grown out and it shows."

The men left the Prater Farm and drove directly to the sorghum patch where they found the missing mule! After the men caught the mule, a black man who worked for the man stopped him and said—

"I want to see if that white spot is in his mane." He pulled the mule's head down, and sure enough, there was the white spot on the mule's mane.

Upon the discovery, the black man stated with conviction---

"Lord, I ain't never gonna do nothin' wrong again, because that white man could tell somebody about it."

See No Evil

Tricking Seymour Prater

Once upon a time, there was a man who owned a hardware store in Vardaman, Mississippi where robberies continued to happen. The man had not been successful in finding out who was taking things from his store. Having heard about Seymour Prater, the man, his friend, and his son, Hank saddled up their horses and rode forty miles to the Woodland Community in Pontotoc County.

When the men reached the Woodland Road that led to the Prater Farm, the men turned onto the road and saw that there were many hog pens that bordered the driveway and the road. There was also a small hill along the drive leading to the Prater farmhouse, hiding the view of the house.

Hank decided to test Seymour Prater. He pulled the saddle off his horse and laid it over in the hog pen. When the men arrived at the house, Mr. Prater's wife told them that Seymour was down the hillside cutting wood. This location put Seymour Prater completely out of view of the men when they arrived at the drive.

When they found Prater moments later, Hank's dad told Mr. Prater that someone had stolen his saddle and asked if he could tell them who it was. Mr. Prater then closed his eyes and rubbed his forehead and said—

"Yes, I can see your saddle. It's lying in my hog pen where you came off the Woodland Road, and an ole' sow is chewing on the leather right now."

Hank said his dad told him to go get the saddle! His dad then told Mr. Prater the real reason for their visit was because someone was stealing goods from his hardware store. Seymour then described an individual whom Hank's dad had already suspicioned as the thief. He described the man's height, weight, color of his hair, and color of his eyes! He also told them about an old logging road and an empty, dilapidated house located two miles north of Vardaman where some of the stolen goods were stored. The men recognized the location being described and later stopped by there on their way home. They were able to recover some of the stolen goods just as Seymour Prater had told them.

L. Sydney Fisher

The Serial Pet Poisoner

Once upon a time, a little boy named Ray had a dog that he loved very much. One day, he found the dog dead. Unable to make sense out of the mystery death, Ray's father decided to travel from Amory, Mississippi to Pontotoc where he would seek the help of Seymour Prater, the man reputed to "see more" than other folks.

Seymour Prater told Ray's father, Bob that his neighbor had poisoned the dog, but he said that the little boy "would get another dog that was smart enough to not get poisoned or die by any other means but would instead die of old age".

Mr. Prater's prediction proved correct after the little boy got a dog that was very smart and died of old age.

Sometime later, Ray's dad, Bob had a cat named Micky that he loved very much. The cat

See No Evil

would lie around his neck when he was working in his garden. He also had a cow and kept his cow feed in a barrel in the barn.

One day, he began to notice that the cow feed was disappearing. He figured it must be a rat and decided to set a huge rat trap in the barrel. He buried the rat trap a few inches in the feed to conceal it. Later the next day, Bob noticed that his neighbor had his hand bandaged. He asked the neighbor what had happened to his hand, but the neighbor refused to tell him. Bob told him that it "looked like he got it caught in a rat trap". The man got mad and left.

Within a day or two later, Bob's cat, Micky was dead. Bob then sought Seymour Prater's help in finding out what had happened to his cat. Mr. Prater then told him that his neighbor, the same man who had poisoned his son's dog, had also poisoned his cat.

L. Sydney Fisher

The Majorette's Ring

Once upon a time in 1938, a majorette in the New Albany High School Band placed a diamond ring on a window sill in the band hall while she went outside to practice twirling her baton. When she came back inside, the ring had disappeared.

A few days later, the majorette then visited Seymour Prater. After a few minutes of quiet time, Mr. Prater responded—

"I see-- I see a tall, slender boy who appears stooped when he walks. Or, he more shuffles than walks, and never looks anyone in the eye when he talks to them."

The majorette knew exactly who Mr. Prater was describing and went back to New Albany where she confronted the boy.

See No Evil

Unfortunately, he denied taking the ring, and she was never able to prove the theft.

L. Sydney Fisher

The Runaway Bride

In the summer of 1934, Jessie Prater, the daughter of Seymour Prater was living in Hattiesburg, Mississippi but was scheduled to begin teaching school later in the fall in Tupelo, Mississippi. Jessie's fiancé, Lavell, had just gotten out of school and did not have a job.

The couple traveled to Ellisville, Mississippi and decided to get married in the Baptist Parsonage. They kept their marriage a secret but only told Jessie's twin, Bessie who vowed not to mention it to anyone. Later when Jessie returned home from summer school, she walked into the Prater farmhouse where her father, Seymour Prater confronted her. Jessie said that he looked at her with those "keen blue eyes and said—

"Jessie, you are married." The expression on Seymour Prater's face was a look that she recognized when her father was certain of himself.

Jessie did not lie outright but tried to dodge the conversation by telling Mr. Prater that he "couldn't believe everything that he heard", but he must have known the truth because he never mentioned it again. Months later during Thanksgiving dinner, Jessie told the rest of the family about her elopement while away at summer school.

L. Sydney Fisher

The Sleeping Prophet
&
The Mississippi Mystic
The Divinely Gifted

Edgar Cayce

See No Evil

Edgar Cayce was born on March 18, 1877 in Kentucky. Like Seymour Prater who was ten years older than him and born a Southern boy in Alabama on April 21, 1867, he possessed extraordinary powers that were beyond any logical explanation. Cayce's first introduction to his supernatural ability came to him as a young boy in May, 1889. He was hidden inside a wood hut, deep in a Kentucky forest where he was quietly reading the Bible.

At that moment, he was visited by a woman messenger with wings who told him that his prayers had been heard and were now going to be answered. She told him that his gifts would be discovered as he slept. Prophecies, healing cures, and metaphysical information was provided to him by an unknown source while Cayce was in a nocturnal trance.

It's unknown if Seymour Prater ever knew Edgar Cayce or heard his name, but the two men seemed to lead similar paths during their lifetimes, and it makes for an intriguing discussion.

Like Cayce, Seymour Prater also encountered a divinely appointed man who delivered an important message to him as a young boy. The man told Prater how to develop his gifts of clairvoyance, and Prater practiced the messenger's advice for the remainder of his life.

Both Cayce and Prater were clairvoyants. A clairvoyant is someone who can "see" things, people, or events which are hidden. While there is no concrete scientific evidence for how the supernatural ability works, clairvoyants have been credited with finding missing children and lost objects. Today, neuroscientists are dedicating more time to studying this psychic phenomena.

Seymour Prater and Edgar Cayce both lived in Alabama, just 70 miles apart during their early years. However, Prater left Alabama and moved to Mississippi by 1880. While Cayce worked as a photographer in Selma, Alabama for many years, Prater worked as a detective in Texas before settling in Pontotoc, Mississippi where he was a successful farmer.

Another interesting event in the men's lives was the timing of their marital commitments. On April 11, 1897, Seymour Prater married Rachel Lee Roye. Just one month earlier on March 14, 1897, Edgar Cayce became engaged to Gertrude Evans, the woman whom he would pledge devotion and undying love for the remainder of his life.

Edgar Cayce and Seymour Prater both had blue eyes. According to research over the last decade, there appears to be a significant degree of psychic ability in people with blue eyes or light colored eyes. It's not known why this phenomena appears in subjects with light colored eyes, but it has been documented. A book titled, *The Children of Now* by Dr. Meg Blackburn Losey is an interesting and compelling read that discusses this occurence.

Subjects who display clairvoyant abilities have also been found to have an enlarged area of the brain that is not typical in others without any known psychic skills. This finding is discussed in my book (Chapter 4, page 53), **The Phoenix Mission**, a book inspired by the U.S. Army's psychic spy program, Stargate.

People born with psychic abilities like Cayce and Prater are commonly known to be left-handed or ambidextrous. While it's true that everyone has a level of psychic ability or can learn to be more psychic, there is evidence that some people are more psychic than others, and it could be genetic.

Prater was known for being able to tap into his mental powers by closing his eyes. During a session with Seymour Prater, he instructed the querent not to speak while he placed his fingertips against his eyelids or temples. He asked the querent a few questions regarding the person or object that they were seeking information about before he closed his eyes to "see" the answer. The answers came to him in the form of images, like pictures on a movie reel.

He never provided the name of any person whom he indicated was involved in a crime or other event. Prater only gave descriptions of the people involved, but his descriptions were always in color. His visions were detailed and often involved multiple time references in which he was able to see a past event and predict a future outcome.

Prater and Cayce were equally religious and spiritual men who loved God and practiced Christianity. Both of the men proclaimed that their gift came from God, and neither of them ever accepted monetary payment for their supernatural help.

Seymour Prater was renowned across the southeast and as far north as New York. Like Cayce who became famous and a national sensation, Prater helped thousands of people during his lifetime. Considering how many lives were impacted from these two men whose paths seemed to intersect, it would seem probable for them to have known of each other, and yet there is no proof of that.

Days before his death, Edgar Cayce said that he would be buried on January 5, 1945. He died on January 3, 1945 and was buried on the exact same day that he had predicted. Cayce died of complications of a stroke. He was 67 years old.

Almost four months later, the 78 year-old mystic, Seymour Prater, died on his birthday April 21, 1945. He passed away as a patient at the Pontotoc Clinic where he had been treated for a brain tumor. Both men with the extraordinary mental gift of clairvoyance died from brain disorders within the same year, just months apart.

After studying the life of Edgar Cayce and Seymour Prater, an undiscovered clairvoyant match to Cayce, I am convinced that Prater was destined to leave behind a supernatural legacy that must be shared. Were the two men divinely appointed and born ten years apart on purpose? Were the men's life journeys so similar that they were intended to cross paths somewhere along the way? Or, were they both just supernatural wonders living separate lives who provided an uncanny sense of comfort and healing?

There is a certainty that cannot be denied. It is unquestionable that both men possessed a supernatural ability that modern day science cannot explain, and it is this legacy that still influences today's esoteric studies and neuroscientific research. In a world of supernatural wonders, paranormal experiences, and unexplained mysteries, the last question that I leave here is...Do YOU believe?

Have you heard about this story?

Now a #1 Bestseller on Amazon!

L. Sydney Fisher

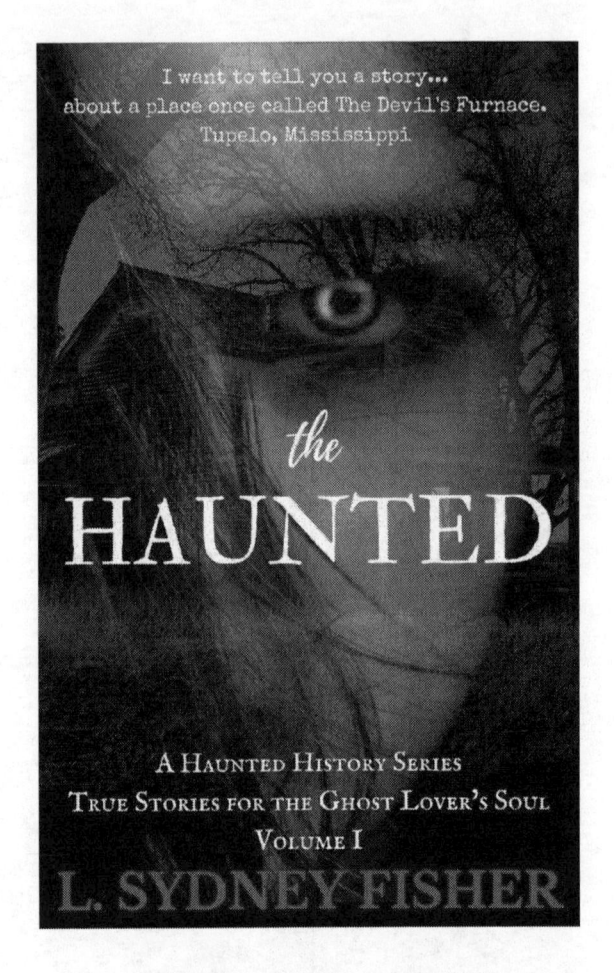

The Haunted

A Collection of TRUE Stories
for the Ghost Lover's Soul
Volume I

Made in the USA
Columbia, SC
29 August 2017